The
Coral
Reef Aquarium

An Owner's Guide To

A HAPPY HEALTHY FISH

Howell Book House

Howell Book House

A Pearson Education Macmillan Company

1633 Broadway

New York, NY 10019

Macmillan Publishing books may be purchased for business or sales promotional use. For information, please write to: Special Markets Department, Macmillan Publishing USA, 1633 Broadway, New York, NY 10019.

ISBN: 1-58245-117-6

Library of Congress Cataloging-in-Publication Data

Shimek, Ron L.

The coral reef aquarium: an owner's guide to a happy healthy fish / [Ron L. Shimek].

p.   cm.

Includes bibliographical references (p.   ).

1. Marine Aquariums.   2. Coral reef animals.   I. Title.

SF457.1.S545   1999

639.34'2—dc21   99-25667

                              CIP

Manufactured in the United States of America

10 9 8 7 6 5 4 3 2 1

Series Director: Amanda Pisani

Book Design: Michele Laseau

Cover Design: Iris Jeromnimon

Illustration: Ron Shimek, Ph.D.

Photography: Scott W. Michael and Janine Cairnes-Michael

Production Team: Carrie Allen, Oliver Jackson, Faunette Johnston, Clint Lahnen, Dennis Sheehan, Terri Sheehan

Contents

Understanding
the

part one

Coral Reef

chapter 1

An Artificial Ecosystem

So you want to set up a reef aquarium. Well, you are not alone. The beauty and diversity of the coral reefs have captivated people for a long time. Setting up a marine reef aquarium is not particularly hard. After all, you just need some animals, a tank, some salt water and presto! You have created a

marine reef aquarium. Keeping your animals healthy, however, is a bit more involved. There are numerous ways to successfully establish a marine reef aquarium, although many of these methods are exceptionally technically complex. Such complex methods, however, are no more successful than a more basic approach that deals with the organisms and the system as if they were components of an ecosystem as, indeed, they are. I will follow the basic approach in this book. It is an approach that works, and it is relatively inexpensive. It has the further advantage of producing a resilient system that is easy to maintain.

A Bit of Necessary Biology

An ecosystem consists of a physical environment, organisms and definite and repeatable pathways for energy and material transfer. We refer to these pathways as "food chains" or "food webs." In recognizing that animals must feed, we are recognizing the fundamental biological truth of the necessity of energy and material transfer. Organisms eat to obtain energy for their metabolic pathways and to obtain materials to build or repair tissues. For the vast majority of organisms, this energy source is the sun. Organisms that can use the sun to power their synthetic machinery are plants, algae and photosynthetic bacteria called cyanobacteria, or blue-green algae.

These organisms capture the energy in sunlight using a special pigment (chlorophyll), and they use this energy to combine carbon dioxide (CO_2) and water (H_2O) molecules into a sugar called glucose. This process is known as photosynthesis. Oxygen gas, O_2 is given off as a byproduct of this reaction. Later, to power other cellular processes, this sugar can be slowly broken back down to its constituent carbon dioxide and water molecules, and the stored energy in it can be recovered. This process is called respiration, and it uses oxygen to burn the sugar.

Organisms are not very efficient at utilizing the food they eat. As a rule, only about 10–20 percent of the eaten food is converted into animal tissue. The rest is lost as waste, undigested food, respiration byproducts or waste energy (heat). The moral for the reef aquarist is that animals need to feed, and because the animals are inefficient at utilizing food, they must be fed a lot to remain in good health.

In maintaining a mini-reef aquarium as an artificial ecosystem, the movement of all this material and chemical energy through the various ecological systems is facilitated. This in turn facilitates the stability of the system and the final removal of excess products from the system.

This might sound complicated and complex, but in practice, it is easy to construct and even easier to maintain. These artificial ecosystems are designed to allow you to sit back and enjoy the system without worrying about constant adjustments and maintenance. Most aquarists can maintain such a system with as little as a few easily scheduled hours of care per week.

Natural Versus Artificial Habitats

To be a fully functional ecosystem, your captive reef must contain analogues of all the components of natural reef ecosystems. There are two significantly different types of components in our systems: the water and the substrate. The water, not surprisingly, consists of the fluid water medium with its dissolved and suspended solids and the organisms found in it. These organisms may be rather arbitrarily defined as swimming or planktonic organisms. Swimming organisms are organisms that are able to move significant distances against water currents using their own locomotion. Generally, we place most fishes, squid, marine mammals and some of the larger swimming crustaceans and snails in this category. Planktonic organisms are organisms that are pretty much at the whim of the water currents,

> **ANIMALS NOT MEANT FOR THE HOME AQUARIUM**
>
> Note that truly mid-water or pelagic species, whether fish or invertebrates, are effectively impossible to keep in tanks smaller than 1,000 gallons. So if your heart is set on maintaining a pelagic shark, jack or jellyfish, you had best find a job as an aquarium technician at a large commercial aquarium and give those urges an outlet there. Such animals have no place in the typical home aquarium because you simply cannot provide conditions for even short-term survival of most of these species.

although they might be able to swim some rather considerable distances, particularly in relation to their body

7

size. These are rather sloppy definitions (broadly based on size), but they work pretty well in most cases.

Water in Nature Versus Water in the Artificial System

The water environment in your artificial system is the most abnormal of all the environments in captive ecosystems. This is primarily because it is severely limited in size relative to the hard substrate in the tank. Much of the food and raw materials necessary in a natural coral reef are brought to the reef through the action of water currents. Relative to the size of the reef at any place and time, the volume of the ocean is immense and contains an effectively unlimited supply of food and raw chemical materials. In nature, such materials are never depleted because they are renewed, literally, with the next wave.

Fish that dwell near the reef are known as epibenthic animals (Spot lionfish, Pterois antennata).

The very small volume of water in even the largest of our systems comprises only a very small fraction of the amount of water passing over the same amount of reef substrate in nature. This means that our systems can become rapidly and seriously depleted in both materials and food. Because neither of these conditions typically is encountered in nature, the animals have no contingency behavioral responses to the conditions of insufficient food and dissolved essential chemicals. Monitoring and maintaining these materials is the major duty necessary to maintain a healthy artificial ecosystem.

The water environment is important for another reason, of course. It is the home of many of the fish species we keep in our systems. Maintenance of the appropriate water conditions is critical for the well-being of these animals.

ANIMALS LIVING NEAR THE REEF

Most of our fishes fall into the category of epibenthic animals. These animals are found near the hard reef substrate but not on it. Under normal conditions in the real world, they might be found as far from the reef as a few meters, but they are not really ever found in mid-water. At night, most of these individuals find shelter in a hole or nook in the reef and huddle up to pass the night in safety.

ANIMALS LIVING ON THE SUBSTRATE

Organisms that live on or in the substrates are referred to as benthic organisms. Benthic organisms live on or in the bottoms of bodies of water. The animals that live on the surface of the substrate are referred to as epifaunal organisms or epifauna. The epifauna can be mobile such as crabs or sea anemones, or they can be immobile such as corals. Many epifaunal animal species make good aquarium inhabitants, and a few of them are necessary to main-

tain a healthy tank. Epifaunal hermit crabs, for example, are mostly scavengers and help keep the tank clean of uneaten food. In addition, many of the epifaunal gastropods are exceptionally good grazers on microalgae and are useful in helping keep the sides of the tank clean.

Corals live on the substrate's surface and are known as epifaunal animals.

ANIMALS LIVING IN THE SUBSTRATE

Organisms that live in the substrates are known as infauna. The infauna can be found in either rocks or sediments. The majority of the living tissue found in natural systems are forms of algae. Algae are plant-like photosynthetic organisms. Although a few algae are related closely to green plants, most are not, and all differ significantly in structure from the common green plants with which we are familiar. About 80 percent of the biomass (or mass of living tissue) found on a coral reef is comprised of algae of one type or another. Many of these algae are visible on the surface of the reef, but a substantial component lives inside coral rock and reef rubble. In addition, many animals, particularly several varieties of worms and clams, are adapted to bore into rocks, constructing burrows where they live. On normal reef rock, there might be as many as 35,000 to 50,000 worms per square meter of surface area.

In normal reef environments, infaunal organisms can easily be found at depths within the substrate exceeding several meters. Obviously, in our sediment-limited tanks, they can only go down a fraction of that distance. Nonetheless, maintaining a healthy sediment for infauna in our artificial ecosystems is one of the major keys to successful reef-keeping.

The reef environment is home to a variety of organisms that live in the substrate; these are known as infauna. Infauna include algae and worms (pink feather duster worm).

Interdependent Habitats

We need to keep each of these separate habitats as a successful and functional part of our artificial ecosystem to maintain the system for any reasonable length of time. The techniques necessary to do this are the basis for this book and will be covered in detail in subsequent chapters. All the various components of an ecosystem are interconnected and interdependent, of course, and that interdependence is the key to success with reefs. The various components automatically assist the reef-keeper in correcting mistakes and in buffering the system against deleterious changes.

In our tanks, we set up a substantially complex system that will automatically work—once we give it the correct conditions. This system, in turn, becomes more stable and less demanding with time. In effect, the longer a reef is set up, the easier it is to keep it going. Not a bad trick!

A basic difference to remember between natural reef ecosystems and our captive ones is the scale of the various components. In our small systems, we trade off the size and expense of a large mimic of a natural system with a small analogue that doesn't work quite as well but is still a good system.

In the natural reef environment, the inhabitants are interdependent.

The lack of long-term stability in the home reef should be the single major concern of aquarists. I am not referring to a stability of chemical reactions or salinity; even in nature, these chemical components of the reef environment can and do fluctuate significantly. Rather, I mean a stability of the organism components of the systems. In nature *and* in our ecosystems, it is the *organisms and not the aquarists* that govern and maintain chemical levels. The aquarist needs to monitor that maintenance and to tweak it whenever necessary to keep it within acceptable ranges.

You must make up for the deficiencies caused by the small size of the system by monitoring and adjusting it either by direct or indirect manipulation. Direct manipulation, for example, would include maintaining salinity within a proper range by adding water to replace any that has evaporated from the system. Indirect manipulation would be characterized by monitoring the sand bed periodically and by adding necessary organisms if the system seems a bit off kilter.

chapter 2

Chemical

Considerations

One common misconception is that managing a reef aquarium takes a significant amount of effort in the realm of chemical management. It certainly is possible to manage a reef aquarium in such a manner, and it can be done successfully. Such an approach is truly micromanagement of the system, however, and I do not believe it is a good mini-reef practice. It is much easier to delegate the management responsibilities to some of the organisms in the system, with an occasional tweak from the ecosystem manager (you). On the other hand, the reefkeeper needs to be aware of some of the chemical properties of his system.

So, while it is necessary to know some chemical considerations and to understand the results of some common chemical reactions, it is not necessary to know all the detailed chemistry occurring in your system. In fact, it is impossible. The discipline of chemical oceanography has developed to understand the complex and varied chemistry occurring in seawater. Although some reactions are well understood as individual reactions, how these reactions change in water solutions containing many chemicals is still largely a mystery.

The water that is part of a reef's inhabitants is as critical for their survival as the water in which they live.

The first chemical information we need to remember is that we are dealing with a system immersed in water. Water is an amazingly odd and wonderful substance. Water is necessary for all life. All the chemical reactions in any cell take place in the water environment inside that cell.

Water as a Solvent

Water can dissolve anything, at least in small amounts. It is not for nothing that water has been referred to as the universal solvent. A portion of any material in contact with water is dissolved in it.

Because we don't have access to the effectively infinite volume of the world's ocean to flush our tanks of nasty chemicals, we must have methods of either filtering them out, detoxifying them or diluting them. To some extent, we will use all three methods in our reef management.

The Dissolution of Ions

Water is a solvent that facilitates dissolution of what are called ionic materials. This is a five-dollar way of saying that water dissolves salts easily. Ionic materials are formed because of the way atoms are constructed. Atoms are composed of a tiny nucleus surrounded by electrons. In most atoms, these electrons form a cloud surrounding the nucleus. In some elements, these electron clouds are more or less full. This is a peculiarity of the way atoms are different from element to element. If the cloud is mostly full, the atom has a strong affinity for electrons to fill the cloud. If the cloud is mostly empty, the atom can relatively easily loose an electron or two. Whenever one of these changes occurs, the atom becomes an ion. The nucleus of an atom is positively charged, and the electrons each represent a negative charge. If an atom becomes an ion by grabbing an electron to fill its electron cloud, it has an extra negative charge. Similarly, if an atom ionizes by losing an electron, it becomes positively charged.

Although there are types of chemicals in our reef systems that don't form ionic bonds with one another, most of the chemicals we have to worry about *do* form these ionic bonds, and most of them are salts of one sort or another. Common salt, sodium chloride, is represented by the chemical shorthand of "NaCl." The "Na" stands for *"naturtium"*, which is Latin for sodium;, and the "Cl" obviously stands for chloride. Sodium chloride dissolves in water to form salt water by forming ions. The sodium gives up an electron to the chloride, and two ions are formed—Na^+ and Cl^-, respectively.

A peculiarity of ions in solution is that they can react with any other ions of the opposite charge. Because most of the common substances dissolved in seawater form ions, the types of combinations that can occur are really staggering. Not surprisingly, for many reactions, the potential outcomes are not necessarily as clear cut as we would like to portray them. Because oceanic chemistry can be so complex, we generally simplify all this for our weak and feeble minds by discussing only one reaction at a time. In some of my explanations later in the book, however, I will mention a few places in which problems might be caused by inappropriate combinations.

ACID-BASE BALANCING

There is one particular ionic reaction we must be familiar with in great and gory detail—the reaction that occurs when water itself ionizes. Water, H_2O or HOH, can dissociate into two ions: H^+ and OH^- (called hydrogen and hydroxyl ions, respectively). In pure water, this happens very infrequently. Only one of every 10 million atoms ionizes. Written in "scientific notation," the one in 10 million becomes 0.0000001 or 1×10^{-7}. The exponent, -7, indicates the number of spaces to the right of the decimal point that the digit is located.

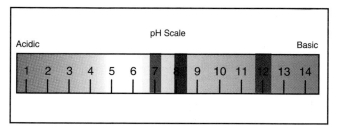

The hydrogen ion concentration is important to the aquarist because it is a measurement of the acidity of a water solution. The more hydrogen ion, the more acid. Now, writing hydrogen ion concentration in scientific or decimal notation is cumbersome and time consuming. Scientists, being at least as lazy as everyone else, devised an index to indicate the relative acidity of solutions using a quicker method. Simply put, this index involves taking the exponent of the hydrogen ion concentration, making the sign positive and using that number as a measure of acidity. So in neutral water, with a hydrogen ion concentration of 10^{-7}, the index value becomes 7. This index has a name, the *per Hydrion* (*Hydrion* = hydrogen ion) value, which is abbreviated as the pH value.

In water solutions, the pH can vary from 1 to 14, indicating very acid to very alkaline solutions, respectively. The pH value of 7 is neutral, being right in the center of the range. It is important to realize that this scale is not linear but logarithmic; each change by 1 pH unit indicates a change in concentration of hydrogen ion by a factor of 10. So a solution with pH 6 is 100 times as acidic as a solution with pH 8. Consequently, changes in pH often are very critical to our ecosystem's success. Normal marine pH varies from about 8.0 to about 8.4.

CRITICAL CHEMISTRY

The single most important series of chemical reactions of which a reef-keeper must be aware concern the relationship between carbon dioxide (CO_2) and the various ions formed by its dissolution in water and the process of calcification.

Carbon dioxide dissolves in water to form bicarbonate (H_2CO_3). Bicarbonate dissociates to form a hydrogen ion (H^+) and bicarbonate ion (HCO_3^-). This, in turn, dissociates into another hydrogen ion and carbonate (CO_3^{-2}) ion. The carbonate ion can combine with calcium ion (Ca^{+2}) to form calcium carbonate. Several things are vitally important about this relationship. First, the source of carbonate for the calcium carbonate comes from carbon dioxide. This carbon dioxide, in turn, comes from the respiration of organisms in the tank. We now have a link from the photosynthesis discussed earlier to the calcification of corals. Second, each step in the chain is reversible.

FOR THE CHEMISTRY NERD IN YOU

A chemist would express the relationship between carbon dioxide, the ions forme by its dissolution in water and the process of calcification as follows:

$$CO_2 + H_2O \leftrightarrow H_2CO_3 \leftrightarrow H^+ +$$
$$HCO_3^- \leftrightarrow H^+ + CO_3^{-2} \leftrightarrow CO_3^{-2} +$$
$$Ca^{+2} \leftrightarrow CaCO_3.$$

The arrows pointing both ways at each step in the reaction indicate that the reactions are reversible.

Chemical reactions such as this can be thought of as a sort of balance. If you add any one of the products or reactants, it will shift the set of reactions to bring that concentration in line with all other products. The addition of CO_2 to this reaction, for example, will tend to force the whole series of reactions to proceed to the right (as set out in the chemical equation), eventually causing an increase in calcification. In doing so, however, it also will produce a number of hydrogen ions, shifting the pH toward the acidic end. Likewise, if the system is becoming more acidic (having more hydrogen ions released) from some other source, this will tend to cause a decrease in the calcification rate or a dissolution of calcium carbonate and a final release of carbon dioxide gas from the system.

For a number of reasons, this reaction is relatively stable. Consequently, minor changes in pH are moderated by the shifts in the relative abundance of all these various ions. This chemical reaction series significantly helps keep the pH in the appropriate range for a coral reef aquarium, and it is said to "buffer" the system against rapid changes. In essence, this series of reactions dampens out or prevents rapid swings in pH.

There are also some other predictable effects. During the day on a real reef (and in the home aquarium), animals respire and algae photosynthesize. Although the respiration produces carbon dioxide, photosynthesis uses

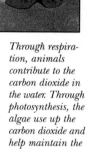

it up faster than it is produced. This means there is less carbon dioxide available to form carbonate ions, which in turn "pulls" the reactions to the left of the equation, which then draws hydrogen ions out of the solution resulting in a rising pH. During the night, both the algae and the animals respire, producing significant amounts of carbon dioxide. This pushes the entire reaction to the right. There is more hydrogen ion, and the pH drops. This cyclical fluctuation of pH from a low value in the morning (as low as about 7.9) to a high value in the evening (up to about 8.4) is normal and is nothing to be concerned about.

Through respiration, animals contribute to the carbon dioxide in the water. Through photosynthesis, the algae use up the carbon dioxide and help maintain the proper pH.

The cyclical nature of the pH is mirrored by other tank chemistry. If you monitor your tank parameters closely, you can definitely detect these variations. It is natural to be concerned when first encountering some of these shifts. For true comparisons, you should test at the same time each day.

Another critical effect of the carbon dioxide dissociation reactions is what they do to calcium concentrations. Calcium carbonate is produced as the skeletal material in many marine invertebrates, among them corals and soft corals. Shifts in pH resulting in an increase in acidity can make it much more difficult for corals and other organisms to form their skeletons, and it might even have the effect of shutting them down. Consequently, it pays to monitor pH regularly and to adjust it as necessary.

Measuring Alkalinity (or Carbonate Hardness)

As previously noted, there is much buffering capacity in this set of reactions. This buffering system is referred to as the "carbonate buffering system of seawater." By measuring alkalinity, you effectively get a reading of the amount of bicarbonate ion in the system. Maintaining the alkalinity in the higher part of the normal range facilitates coral skeleton formation.

When water becomes too acidic, it becomes difficult for corals to form their skeletons.

Two sets of units are used to measure alkalinity. The first is a more standard scientific terminology called milliequivalents per liter (meq/l). The normal reef range for alkalinity on this scale is from 2 to about 2.5. It also is acceptable to push the alkalinity higher in reef aquariums, up to values of 3.5 to 4 meq/l. The other scale for measuring alkalinity is called dKH, and each value is 2.8 times the corresponding meq/l value. If you measure by this scale, the normal range is 5 to about 7 dKH, with the pushed values being from 10 to about 11 dKH. Beginning reef aquarists should probably aim for the high side of normal.

The Calcium Factor

The final chemical parameter involved with this set of reactions is calcium. In shallow-water situations, calcium always is saturated. Depending on other conditions, however, its concentration generally varies from about 375 to more than 425 mg/l. In your aquarium, you generally should try to keep it between about 400 and 450 mg/l or a bit higher. This allows for some usage by organisms while still having a sufficient in-tank concentration.

Coping with the Chemistry

Given that there are several important parameters all rolled into the relationship between carbon dioxide, water and calcium carbonate, it should be obvious that controlling and maintaining appropriate levels of these factors is important. At this point, you might begin to feel apprehensive and wonder whether you shouldn't just get a gerbil. Fortunately, keeping these factors in line is easy and inexpensive and is almost totally self-controlling.

THE BEAUTY OF *KALKWASSER*

Most of the controlling adjustments of the system can be done with regular additions of limewater, or *kalkwasser*, to the system. *Kalkwasser* is a saturated solution of calcium hydroxide, and it can be made by mixing about two tablespoons per gallon of calcium hydroxide powder in fresh water. Calcium hydroxide is relatively insoluble in water, so there should be a little left after mixing. The solution looks like weak skim milk. This is left to settle, and the clear fluid is transferred to a closed container. Calcium hydroxide in a water solution reacts with the carbon dioxide in air to precipitate calcium carbonate. This is how blackboard chalk is made; the precipitate is dried and compressed into chalk. Notably, the term *"kalkwasser"* means "chalk water" in German.

The calcium hydroxide powder used to create *kalkwasser* is available from scientific-supply houses (very expensive), pet stores (even more expensive), mail-order pet stores (expensive) or in the food-processing section of the local supermarket or discount store. In the latter locations, it's called pickling lime and it's cheap. Always check the label to make sure it contains only pickling lime or calcium hydroxide. From such sources, the material is pure because it is made for human consumption, and it certainly is reef-safe. It is likely to be only seasonally available, however, so buy enough for at least a few months.

When you keep corals, you might want to replace all evaporated water with kalkwasser. *Soft corals use calcium carbonate in their skeletons just like stony corals.*

WATER—THE UNIVERSAL SOLVENT

Being a universal solvent has had some interesting ramifications. There used to be a common saying, "The solution to pollution is dilution." To some extent, this is true. If a chemical is toxic in large quantities, one of the ways to make it nontoxic is to dilute the large quantities with lots of water. Pretty soon, you don't have a problem any more. As a result of this rather interesting thinking, the world's oceans now contain most of the industrial pollutants washed downstream out of the rivers. Fortunately, the ocean's volume is vast, and these chemicals are not a general problem. Yet . . .

Kalkwasser can be messy to mix and handle, and it takes some time to let the material clear after mixing. You might eventually want a different way to maintain the appropriate levels. Both calcium and alkalinity levels can be altered independently of one another by using any of a number of regulative additives available at your local fish store or through mail-order outlets. While using such materials, it is imperative that both alkalinity and calcium be tested regularly to make sure they are within normal parameters. Utilizing *kalkwasser* instead maintains all these limits automatically. Once a routine is established, you need only test to reassure yourself of the levels.

Additionally, as you add more corals, you might need to resort to other means of maintaining the correct calcium levels, such as the use of calcium reactors (a somewhat sophisticated procedure and beyond the current scope of this book).

Kalkwasser has a pH of 12 and is caustic. If it is added to an aquarium all at once, it can and will kill some organisms. If it is added slowly, however, it almost performs miracles. If you don't have many organisms that utilize calcium from your tank's water, you probably can get by with testing the system for calcium periodically and adding *kalkwasser* as needed. If you have a lot of corals, soft corals or other organisms that withdraw calcium from the water to produce their skeletons, you might need to replace all evaporated water with *kalkwasser*. In such situations, there are two inexpensive ways to add the material.

Adding Kalkwasser with a Sump Dispenser

If you have a large sump for your system, you also have an almost foolproof method for adding *kalkwasser*. In this situation, you need a large (2–5 gallon) narrow-mouthed jar or bottle. Construct a stand for the bottle that supports it in an inverted position with the aperture down. The height of the stand should be adjusted to maintain

The sump dispenser for kalkwasser *is an easy way to maintain the appropriate water level and calcium concentration.*

the normal sump-water level just above the mouth of the jar. The jar then should be filled with *kalkwasser* and inverted onto its stand. As water evaporates out of the system, the water level in the sump will drop until it gets below the mouth of the jar. At that time, a bubble will go up into the jar, and *kalkwasser* will rush out and mix with the sump water. Enough kalkwasser will flow out to fill the sump a bit beyond the level of the jar. This will stop the transfer of *kalkwasser* until

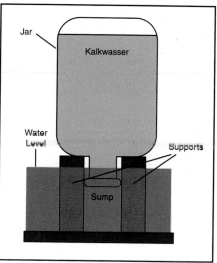

Jar

Kalkwasser

Water
Level

Supports

Sump

evaporation takes the level down again. This method has the advantage of being self-regulating and easy to build. It can, however, be cumbersome and difficult to maneuver big bottles of *kalkwasser* around in the confines of the sump.

Adding Kalkwasser with an Adjustable Container

The second inexpensive way to dose *kalkwasser* requires the purchase of a container with attached tubing that contains an intravenous fluid thumb-switch regulator. The *kalkwasser* should be placed in the container and allowed to drip into the main system. The regulator valve can be adjusted to allow the material to drip in at a rate of one drop every second or two, or it can be adjusted to some other value that matches the evaporation rate.

Oh No, Now Nitrogen!

Algae use ammonium in the course of protein synthesis, so you shouldn't have to worry about ammonia build-up in your tank.

Most of the Earth's atmosphere consists of nitrogen, as is most of the gas dissolved in water. We totally ignore this because nitrogen gas is biologically inert. Nitrogen is an absolute necessity for life, however, because it comprises a significant amount of protein, nucleic acids and other important biologically active compounds. Nitrogen generally enters animal metabolism as protein subunits called amino acids. When proteins are digested, they are broken down into their constituent amino acids, which then are resynthesized into other proteins or are modified into other compounds. Likewise, when protein is metabolized, it is first subdivided into an amino acid, which then is broken into its constituent parts. One common component of all amino acids is the ammonia group that gives amino acids their name.

Ammonia is a gas made from one nitrogen atom bonded to three hydrogen atoms, and it has the chemical formulation of NH^{3-}. Ammonia is very soluble in water, where it combines with a water molecule to form ammonium (NH^{4+}) and hydroxyl (OH^-) ions. In biological systems, free ammonia is never found, but ammonium ion is the common byproduct of protein breakdown. As it turns out, ammonia gas is exceptionally toxic, and ammonium ion is only less so. Consequently, all organisms have ways of removing ammonium ion from their bodies. In small organisms, it can simply diffuse across the surface of the animal. In most animals, however, it is actively secreted as a urine.

Excretion of ammonia is exceptionally important for animals; if it doesn't occur efficiently, they die. Because ammonium ion is very soluble in water, the general solution is to flush it out of the body into "the great outdoors." In this case, the virtually infinite volume of water washes it away and rapidly dilutes it. At least, that's how it works in nature. In our reefs, however, it's another story.

Ammonium ion is required by many plants and algae as a nitrogen source for their protein synthesis. After an aquarium is well established, most free ammonia is sequestered by algae or bacteria within a few seconds of its release. In these situations, unless something goes drastically wrong, you really never need to worry about ammonia concentrations.

KEY CYCLING TIMES

Ammonium generally is a concern to aquarists in two situations. The first occurs when the reef system is just set up, before the biological filter has reached full operational capacity. You'll learn more about the biological filter a bit later, but suffice it to say that the biological filter converts ammonia and other nitrogenous compounds (such as nitrates and nitrites) to nitrogen gas.

During this initial setup, the system typically passes through a several-week period in which there is a relatively high concentration of ammonia. This eventually drops off and is replaced by a period in which there is a lowered concentration of ammonia but a high concentration of nitrite. This, in turn, is replaced by a period in which ammonia drops to unmeasurable levels. The nitrite also fades away, being replaced by a relatively high concentration of nitrate ion. This, too, eventually drops to low levels. This sequence of various nitrogenous ionic compounds is referred to as the nitrogen cycle, and a tank in the midst of it is said to be "cycling."

During the cycling process, the aquarist must suppress the urge to fully stock the system. Generally, a few animals are added during this period, and they function rather like the canaries in coal mines of yore. If you have a particularly large tank, a somewhat greater number of animals can be added (and can even help the maturation of the filter). Remember, however, that this is a delicate time for your system. Ammonium is very toxic, but some hardy fishes can withstand low concentrations of it. Nitrite is still toxic but much less so than ammonium. Finally, nitrate is not toxic at all, but it is an algal fertilizer. Eventually, the biological filter will be able to maintain all these chemicals at a low level as it produces nitrogen gas, which will bubble out of the system.

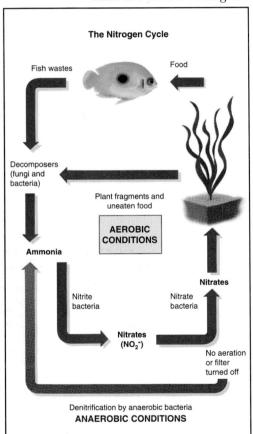

The Nitrogen Cycle

Fish wastes

Food

Decomposers (fungi and bacteria)

Plant fragments and uneaten food

AEROBIC CONDITIONS

Ammonia

Nitrite bacteria

Nitrate bacteria

Nitrates

Nitrates (NO$_2^-$)

No aeration or filter turned off

Denitrification by anaerobic bacteria
ANAEROBIC CONDITIONS

The second period of concern for ammonium spikes is when something large dies in the tank or when a piece of live rock or other material cures in the system. The word "cure" here is a euphemism for rotting. When live rock is collected from the real world, it has a lot of life on it. Much of that life dies during the collection, transport and acclimation phases in a new aquarium. The death and decomposition of such material is referred to as curing. A large reef aquarium typically has a significant capacity for handling the chemicals produced during this process. There's always the chance for an ammonium ion spike, however, a short duration blast of high ammonium concentration. Given the sensitivity of many organisms, such a spike can cause mortality. This is the paradox of nitrogen; it is absolutely necessary for life, yet in waste products it can be lethal to life. The biological filter is our means of maintaining nitrogen ion concentrations at low and tolerable levels.

Finally, Phosphate

Phosphorus, in the form of phosphate ion, is yet another of the essential materials of life that has negative consequences in high concentrations. In our aquarium animals, phosphorus is found in proteins and in some skeletons. Fish bones are composed of calcium phosphate as are some invertebrate shells. Phosphate finds its way into our systems in foods, in excretory products of some animals and by the decomposition of either animals or plants.

Animals excrete phosphate into the water. Because your aquarium undoubtedly will contain more animals than would naturally live in the same volume of water in nature, phosphate must be removed from the tank.

In natural systems, phosphate is an essential mineral nutrient that is in short supply, and this lack of phosphate limits the growth of bacteria and algae. Except in areas of pollution, it always is in short supply. Evolution, therefore, has given these organisms aggressive ways of sequestering and utilizing phosphate.

As previously indicated, in our artificial reefs, there is far less water in relationship to the hard substrate than is found in nature. Nonetheless, we often keep more animals, particularly fish, in this water than would be found in a corresponding volume of water in nature. Not terribly surprisingly, this leads to a build-up of phosphate and other ions in the water. In low or even moderate concentrations, phosphate ion by itself is neither toxic nor harmful. It is, however, a significant stimulant for algal growth and is probably the major cause of reef outbreaks of almost any type of problem algae. In high concentrations, phosphate ion has been implicated in causing a reduction in calcification of corals.

Phosphate, therefore, is a problem for reef aquarists, and it must be removed from the system. Phosphate can be exported from the system in four ways. First, in either the sump or the main aquarium, the growth of some algae can be encouraged. The algae can be periodically harvested, resulting in the removal of significant excess phosphate and nitrates now disguised as plant tissue. In my own aquarium, I harvest some excess algae every two weeks or so. Second, the system can be set up so the *kalkwasser* drips directly into the air injector of a skimmer. This causes the precipitation of fine particles of calcium phosphate into the skimmate, which is removed from the system. Third, you can place phosphate-reducing chemicals (which generally are enclosed in pads) in the sump. These absorb phosphate from the water and then can be discarded. Fourth, the water of the system can be changed periodically, thereby fractionally reducing the phosphate by the proportion of the water removed.

Phosphate control, however, also requires the sequestering and removal of phosphate from the water by organisms. These organisms pass the phosphate along the food chains until it can again be either exported or reused. The concept of material and energy transfer through the aquarium is discussed in the next chapter.

Material and

Energy Flow

In the coral reef ecosystem, solar energy is converted into chemical energy by the action of "producers" such as phytoplankton, algae and zooxanthellae. All other organisms are "consumers" and must eat either producers or producer byproducts. The pathway of energy and

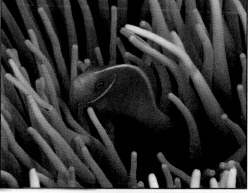

materials through an ecosystem is called a food web. This passage through the system is *not* efficient. For example, when a coral utilizes the by-products of its internal zooxanthellae, only about 10–20 percent of these products are converted into coral or coral products. The rest leave the coral as diffused gases, such as carbon dioxide, or as waste. Similar ratios hold for any energy transfer such as a fish eating plankton or a deposit-feeding worm eating a piece of detritus. In all cases, the efficiency is low. Eventually in a food web, the amount of food remaining of an initial amount is too low to support another transfer of energy. The matter remains in the system, however, and after a while this starts to create problems.

Creating a Food Web in the Coral Reef Aquarium

In our aquariums, we short-circuit some of the food webs by supplying food. This compresses the plankton end of the web. At least some version of all other pathways found in the normal ecosystem is found in the aquarium. We must make sure these pathways function normally to prevent the pollution problems that occur when there is an excessive accumulation of dissolved nutrients or detritus.

On a natural reef, and in our tanks, algal growth is facilitated by dissolved organic materials. This is due to the feeding of animals all along the food chain. This suggests that the obvious solution to nutrient build-up is to reduce either the amount of food offered or the frequency of feeding (or both). Probably the most widespread misinterpretation of biological processes found in the reef aquarium hobby relates to the function of the zooxanthellae in their host animals. This relationship has fostered the following *incorrect* statement. "Corals and many other organisms have symbiotic algae or zooxanthellae in their tissues to produce food for them, and these symbionts should provide sufficient nutrition for the host." If this statement were true, feeding could be kept to a minimum, and the problems of nutrient accumulation would be minimized.

However . . .

Some aquarists tend to forget that corals are predatory animals. In fact, of all the predators on the Earth's surface, corals have the largest percentage of their body devoted to food capture. If the food collected in this way was not important to them, natural selection would have optimized them to utilize other energy sources.

Corals Need to Be Fed

Corals need a lot of nutrients on a daily basis. Much of what they consume goes to mucus production. About 40 percent of the material obtained each day by the corals from their symbiotic zooxanthellae is lost from the animal as dissolved or sloughed mucus. This means corals are "snot factories" filling your tank with dissolved mucus. Much the same happens with any algae in the system, and both processes significantly increase the dissolved nutrients in the aquarium.

The zooxanthellae found in small polyp stony corals provide some of the coral's nutrition.

Corals capture their food using explosive capsules secreted by some of their cells. Corals, sea anemones and soft corals have a lot of them—up to 10,000 per square millimeter or about 6.5 million per square inch. Moreover, they need lots of both raw materials and energy to produce their skeletons. You must remember that the coral skeleton is not just calcium carbonate, it contains a significant amount of organic material in the form of a matrix on which the mineral is deposited.

All these materials, from mucus to the organic matrix of the skeleton to the basic coral tissues, require proteins. The zooxanthellae can produce sugars that power the metabolism of the corals. They also can produce some of the necessary amino acids and the necessary proteins. For the production of the amino acids and proteins, however, they need a source of dissolved nitrogen. Some of this can come from ammonium or nitrate ions in the aquarium water, but most has to come from the digestion of food by the host.

The bottom line is that corals must feed! Based on numerous studies, it appears that, in nature, about 70 percent of a coral's nutritional needs can be met by the zooxanthellae. Predation meets about 25 percent of the needs, and about 5 percent are met by the absorption of dissolved organic materials. These needs are *not* trivial. Corals need a lot of nutrition to survive. In our captive ecosystems, in which light intensities generally are not as great as in natural situations, feeding is even more important.

One type of coral that harbors no zooxanthellae is Tubastrea. *Obviously, the hobbyist must take special care to feed these corals well.*

How Reefs Feed in Nature

The animal-algal symbiosis common in reef areas is a solution to the problem of insufficient high-quality nutrients. One of the statements often bantered about is that the water flowing over a coral reef is nutrient poor. This is true—*but only for dissolved nutrients!*

In fact, water passing over a coral reef contains a fair amount of high-quality animal foods. A recent study by Hamner and colleagues (cited in Chapter 8, "Recommended Reading and Resources") provides some interesting data. They looked at a windward reef in a portion of the Great Barrier Reef and calculated the water flow over the reef to be 6,000 cubic meters of water per 1 linear meter of reef crest in 12 hours. If we assume a depth of 1 meter on the reef crest, using U.S. gallons, this is a flow rate of 2,201 gallons per minute. Adjusted to the volume of a 100-gallon aquarium, the water would have a flow rate of 834 gallons per minute. This water brings 416,142 food items, equivalent to 5 ounces of wet weight of food to the reef crest in a 12-hour period. Most of this food is small zooplankton.

Now, fishes get to the food first. There are several layers of plankton-feeding fishes between the ocean and the reef face, and these fish effectively remove all living planktonic organisms during the day. Fish feces, however, and debris from the feeding reach the reef. Assuming a processing efficiency of 10–20 percent, this means 4 to 4½ ounces of debris and dissolved organic material pass through the volume of a 100-gallon tank during the daylight. At night, the fishes are through feeding for the day, and the zooplankton do impact the reef. The total planktonic nutrition arriving at the reef, for a volume of a 100-gallon aquarium, is then 4 to 4½ ounces of debris and dissolved material per day during the daylight and approximately 5 ounces of zooplankton at night.

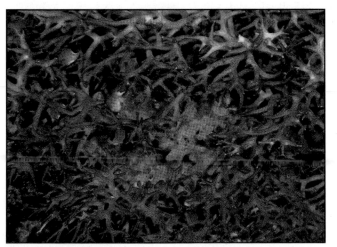

The small polyps of Seriatopora *will snatch up microplankton and other passing debris.*

To simulate this type of natural reef crest environment (in which small polyp stony corals such as *Acropora* predominate), you would feed about 10 ounces (wet weight) of food in a 24-hour period. This is roughly the equivalent of two fast-food hamburgers. *Don't feed your aquarium this much!*

This type of environment, with its high-flow rate of water, is essentially impossible to duplicate in a home aquarium. Furthermore, much of the excess food is washed out of the natural coral reef, and we have no capability to do that in our tanks.

This example illustrates the sheer volume of food hitting a normal reef. Corals with small polyps such as *Acropora*, *Seriatopora* and *Montipora* are found in abundance in such areas. Their small polyps are adapted to catch small particles of debris and microplankton that are there in consistent and constant amounts. Such corals can do well in the home tank if you feed other components of your ecosystem sufficiently. For example, by providing adequate nutrition to the benthos, or bottom dwellers, they in turn will produce particulate prey such as invertebrate larvae or particulate clumps of bacteria for the corals. Large polyp corals, such as *Caulastrea* or *Euphyllia,* need larger prey, and these can be directly fed to the animals by the hobbyist.

Fireworms are segmented worms commonly found in reef aquariums. Most are beneficial scavangers.

The moral of the story is that, even if you don't have a reef crest aquarium, the animals need to be fed—*and fed a lot!* Such feeding of the corals, fishes, shrimps or other animals as well as the herbivory of snails eating algae results in detritus and dissolved organic materials accumulating in the tank. Processing and utilization of detritus and dissolved organic materials is a property of the benthos, particularly the infauna.

Sand-bed Infauna in a Reef Aquarium

Infauna are organisms that live in substrates. The infauna in natural communities include worms, clams, echinoderms such as burrowing sea cucumbers and sea urchins, crustaceans such as amphipods and protozoans (minute single-celled organisms such as amoebas) and bacteria.

The worm diversity in many successful reef tanks typically is lower than the highest diversities found in natural systems but greater than the least diverse. In other words, it's about the middle of the range. Most reef aquariums, however, have far less abundance and diversity than is necessary for a healthy system.

INFAUNA FOR YOU

Bacteria

Bacteria are vitally important because they constitute the biological filter of your aquarium. The different bacteria metabolize different nitrogenous compounds allowing the detoxification and export of nitrogenous animal wastes, such as ammonia, as nitrogen gas. These bacteria only can do this while they are growing, and they grow fastest when uncrowded. Most of the infaunal animals eat bacteria or bacterially covered sediment (which is cleaned of bacteria in the animals' guts). This opens new space for more

---

INFAUNA MAINTENANCE

There should be an appropriate volume of organisms from live sand. Except in the largest of systems, the aquarist should avoid introducing major infaunal predators. This means *no* sand-sifting animals that feed on the organisms in the sediment. You want those sediment-dwelling organisms, so the predators should not be added. On the other hand, burrowing sand swallowers such as sea cucumbers or sea urchins are fine. They disturb the sediments and primarily eat bacteria not animals. It is normal for sand beds to accumulate fine particulate matter. This is mostly fecal pellets, and it is utilized by both the sediment infauna and bacteria as food and substrate.

Siphoning, disturbing or cleaning the sediments will result in significant removal or mortality of sediment organisms and can severely damage the functional aspect of the sand bed. Examining the morphology of both the individual organisms and the whole system allows aquarists to treat their captive reefs as biological systems and to facilitate their maintenance. The role of the benthos in the reef aquarium ecosystem is to maintain energy and material flow through the system, therefore allowing a more normal captive reef to develop.

bacteria and facilitates the nitrogen production. The bacteria never can be totally removed by this predation; they simply reproduce and grow too rapidly. This bacterial reproduction and growth results in the utilization of the dissolved nutrients, such as nitrates and phosphates, and really is the cause of the biological filtration we need.

If the bacteria are not eaten, they tend to grow into patches or masses. Some of the bacteria secrete a material or matrix around themselves. This matrix has a consistency similar to that of rock candy and can quite effectively glue sand grains together. When this occurs in large patches, it can seal off portions of the tank's sand bed from water circulation and can kill all the organisms in it. This can cause a very rapid and very large build-up of nutrients in the reef aquarium system and can subsequently result in the death of many organisms.

The problem of sediment clumping can be simply avoided by maintaining a diverse and abundant association of sediment organisms that will continually eat the bacteria and will physically disturb the sediments.

Shelled Amoebae *(Foraminiferans)*

Shelled amoebae prey on bacteria and thus are necessary for continued bacterial growth. This facilitates the functioning of the biological filter, as the filter works best only when the bacteria in it are actively reproducing.

Worms

Flatworms cruise through the sediments eating detritus and bacteria. They facilitate more energy flow through the system.

Segmented worms (also called polychaete annelids), which are related to the common terrestrial earthworms, are exceptionally common in marine sediments. This is a diverse group containing more than 10,000 species. They are characterized by the presence of tufts of bristles on each side of each segment. The technical term for these bristles is "chaetae," and the term "poly" means many, so the scientific name for these animals can be translated as "many bristles." Aquarists generally call them bristle worms.

Polychaete worms probably are the most numerous and diverse of the visible infauna in most soft-sediment ecosystems, and you should strive for significant diversity in your tank to provide multiple pathways for material flow.

Bristle worms live in the sediment, eat up bacteria and detritus, and produce micro-plankton. In other words, the bristle worm is your friend.

Of particular importance are the scavenging fireworms. These worms are common in the sediments and are juveniles of the common fireworms *Eurythoe* or *Pareurythoe*. Eurythoe is reef safe, an excellent scavenger and an important component of the benthos. Although they can cause irritation when handled, they do not prey on live animals and are good members of the "cleanup" crew.

In addition to being the major detritus-processing component of the benthos, the benthic infaunal bristle worms produce microplankton in the form of reproductive products such as eggs, sperm and larvae. Larval polychaetes can be found in the plankton of my reef system, and they are produced by the reproduction of animals living in the sediments. There also are epibenthic or demersal zooplankton, which can include larvae from annelids but are largely composed of harpacticoid copepods (both animals and their fecal pellets). Harpacticoid copepods are important in the detritus food pathway and they produce fecal pellets used as food by many corals with small polyps as well as other filter feeders.

Algae in the Aquarium

Algae grow easily and can be harvested. In natural systems, the larger predators periodically crop the algae. In our miniature worlds, the aquarist must fulfill that ecological role and periodically harvest excess algal growth. Such algal growth should be encouraged because it is an easy way to remove excess recycled nutrients from a system.

Thus: Algal Removal = Removal of Excess Nutrients.

Infauna and Algae Work Together

The importance of aquarium benthos is that the sediment infauna maintain energy and material flow. Additionally, epibenthic algae provide convenient material export. Healthy and diverse sediment infauna prevent the accumulation of organic material in the sediment, feed the filter-feeding organisms in the system and promote and maintain the biological filter.

The biological filter is maintained by the feeding and movement of the various infaunal animals. When they feed on the filter bacteria, this opens new space on the substrate particles and continually stimulates growth and utilization of dissolved nitrogen and phosphorus compounds. Movement through the sediment aerates the sediment and prevents it from clumping and clogging.

INFAUNA DENSITY

The amount of sediment disturbances caused by a single organism is fairly small, generally ranging from 100 to 200 cubic millimeters (0.006–0.013 cubic inches) per day for small worms. The sediment disturbance caused by all the sediment infauna, however, can be quite considerable. In an aquarium with a well-set-up biological filter and sand bed, the infaunal density should range between 10,000 and 40,000 animals per square meter (or about 1 to 4 animals per square centimeter of sediment surface).

These animals are distributed in a mosaic of patches throughout the bottom of the aquarium and can best be measured by examining the sediment with a magnifying glass where it is visible through the wall near the bottom of the aquarium. Worm tubes and other small organisms will be visible, and you should be able to find 2–10 animals or tubes per linear inch of aquarium wall. These worm and bug densities are perfectly normal and are well within the natural ranges found in equivalent habitats.

A diverse population can include species such as the hard-tubed feather duster.

An infaunal density of 5 tubes per inch of sediment translates into about 2 animals per square centimeter of sediment surface or about 20,000 animals per square meter of aquarium bottom. If each of these worms moves 150 cubic millimeters of bottom per day, the total amount of moved sediment is 4 million cubic millimeters or 4,000 cubic centimeters per day. There are 16.4 cubic centimeters in a cubic inch, so the worm density in such a tank would move about 244 cubic inches. This frequency of movement is sufficient to prevent sediment clumping, and it also provides sufficient time between disturbances for growth and recovery of the sand fauna, bacteria and other organisms.

part two

The
Environment

chapter 4

Necessary

Equipment

Obviously, you can't keep a marine reef without an aquarium, so let's take a look at the fundamental equipment that you'll need.

The Tank

The first piece of equipment you will have to purchase is the aquarium tank itself. Although this might seem like a simple choice, it is not. Standard tanks are available in a number of sizes, shapes and materials.

TANK SIZE

All other things being equal, for a beginner, the larger the tank the better. This is because larger systems have a lot more resiliency built into them. After the system is up and running, it is much harder to cause a large tank to fail than a small one. Under no circumstances should a beginning reef-keeper consider having a tank under about 40 gallons as his first tank.

Nonetheless, large tanks do have some drawbacks. Bigger systems require larger circulation pumps and more lighting. The increase in both the initial and continuing costs can be significant. Both large pumps and higher-powered lights can draw a lot of electrical current. Sometimes the increase in the monthly electric bill can give you pause. Depending on your electric rates, the increase for the installation of a large system can run from about $10 to more than $70 per month.

TANK WEIGHT

Related to a tank's size is its ultimate weight. A 100-gallon tank full of sand, rock and water will weigh in excess of 1,000 pounds and will take up a significant amount of space in the room it's in.

The weight generally is not a problem in most houses, but there are tales of disasters that have occurred when tanks were filled for the first time in poorly constructed houses or apartment buildings. Certain parts of apartment buildings, in particular, are not meant to carry the weight of a large tank. Common sense should dictate tank placement.

PLACEMENT OF THE TANK

Once a tank is set up, it is impossible to move. Be sure to position the tank in such a manner that you can reach all sides and behind it for cleaning and for retrieval of dropped equipment. You might decide after setting up your system to add a new piece of equipment. This will be significantly easier if you considered this possibility prior to the initial setup and left some room behind the tank.

GLASS OR ACRYLIC?

Tanks generally are fabricated from either glass or acrylic plastic. Occasionally you can find fiberglass tanks for sale, and these can work very well. Avoid older used tanks constructed with metal framing. These will corrode and discolor if used for reef tanks. Additionally, they can leach toxic metals back into the tank water.

When deciding between glass and acrylic tanks, you should consider several factors. The first factor is cost. There often is a considerable cost differential between tanks made of these two materials, although the direction of the differential varies depending on the size of the tank and what part of the country you live in.

If the price differential is not significant, other differences between the two types of tanks can help you decide which type you want to purchase.

. *To keep your animals healthy, avoid old tanks with metal frames. Corroding metal can leach toxins into your aquarium's water.*

Glass tanks are significantly heavier than acrylic ones. One person can move an empty 100-gallon acrylic tank without difficulty, but it takes two people to move a glass tank of the same size. Glass is brittle and can break or crack if live rock shifts against it; this is unlikely with acrylic tanks. Acrylic tanks can be drilled to fit aquarium plumbing into them without difficulty or special tools. Glass can be drilled or cut only with difficulty, and this generally means using a professional to do the job. Cutting holes in flat-glass plates that will then be under pressure from the weight of water behind them can cause significant stress if the holes are in the wrong spots. This can cause the glass to crack or break after the tank is filled.

The stiffness of glass, however, has some advantages in the construction of the tanks. Unless the tank is quite large, it seldom needs to be braced to prevent the sides from bowing out. Acrylic tanks always bow outward, sometimes enough to cause noticeable optical distortion. They often have a top plate glued to all sides that acts as a brace to prevent bowing. This is cut with rather small openings in it to insert the tank's contents. These small apertures can cause difficulties in placing rocks in the tank. They also can make reaching to various places in the tank difficult and unpleasant. Acrylic tanks also need support underneath. If a stand is purchased that does not have a complete surface to support the tank, such as metal stands that often just support the tank's edges, a thick piece of plywood should be placed under the tank to prevent the bottom from bowing down and rupturing. For a 100-gallon acrylic tank, the plywood support should be at least ¾-inch thick exterior or marine-grade plywood.

KEEP METALS OUT OF YOUR TANK

As a general rule, no metal should go into the tank. Even stainless steel should be kept out. All metals corrode in salt water, some more rapidly than others. Corrosion releases metal ions into the salt water, and metal ions generally are toxic in all but the smallest concentrations. Copper is particularly lethal and should never be used to treat the diseases of a reef aquarium.

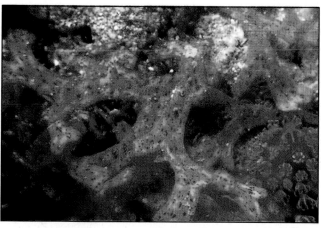

Unsightly algae like to take up residence in scratches on tank walls. This is one good reason to buy a glass tank.

Both glass and acrylic tanks are colored, and this alters the colors of the animals in them. These color changes are slight—the glass is slightly green, the acrylic slightly blue. Most aquarists ignore this, but if you want uncolored glass it is available, although somewhat expensive. Truly uncolored acrylic is not available.

Perhaps the largest drawback of acrylic tanks is the softness of the plastic. Acrylic tanks will scratch on both the outside and the inside. Outside scratches can be buffed out using a soft cloth and toothpaste or acrylic polish. Internal scratches only can be eliminated when the tank is empty and dry. Internal scratches obviously are surface irregularities on the inside of the aquarium wall. Unfortunately, many algae like to grow in such irregularities and will continue to grow in the scratches even after being repeatedly cleaned off. The softness of the acrylic also causes problems with algal removal. It is almost impossible to clean algae off the inside of an acrylic tank for any length of time without scratching the plastic. This in turn facilitates more algal growth, followed by new scratches and even more algal growth. Glass aquariums, on the other hand, can easily be cleaned without scratching the surface.

Although the choice of tank material can be made on the basis of many factors, experienced aquarists often use glass tanks for show or display aquaria and acrylic tanks for sumps, experimental systems, or other areas in which clarity of the walls is not too important.

The Stand

The stand is probably the second most important piece of equipment the aquarist must purchase or make. Surprisingly, many hobbyists give it little forethought. Considering the weight of the tank, however, you should give a lot of thought to what you want holding it up. Additionally, the stand can provide storage for extra equipment, accommodate the sump, house the pumps, and hide the unsightly tangle of pipes and plumbing that characterizes a reef aquarium system. Finally, you want a stand that is visually appealing. Aquariums are beautiful additions to any room, and the stand can contribute significantly to that beauty.

Stands are made from many materials, but the three most common are wood, wood byproducts such as pressed board, and metal. Generally, any of these will work well in the basic process of support. The potential buyer should take several factors into account when deciding on a stand. Most folks forget that keeping a reef aquarium inevitably means the presence of small spills from time to time. Large spills also are common—every experienced hobbyist has tales of "The Big One."

METAL STANDS

Most metal aquarium stands are made of iron or steel that might or might not be well painted. Iron or steel and salt water mean rust. All metal stands will have some rust on them after a while. Although most of this can be removed easily enough or can be prevented with good maintenance, it still happens. Although unsightly, it doesn't cause any problems with the load-bearing capabilities of the stand.

A mini-reef is only beautiful when it's intact. Make sure your aquarium has adequate support.

Metal stands often are the least expensive, and they generally do not have enclosed sides. Metal stands only support the edges of the aquarium. If the aquarium is acrylic, a piece of wood or plywood should be placed between the aquarium and the stand completely supporting the bottom. This also is a good practice for glass tanks that hold more than 75 gallons.

FIBERBOARD STANDS

Stands made of wood byproducts such as fiberboard or pressed board also are common. The surface of these products often is covered with contact paper providing a wood-grain design. Edges often are sealed with a varnish or polyurethane coating to prevent water entry. These products have the advantage of being inexpensive and serviceable.

If spills are rapidly cleaned up, these stands will work well. Hobbyists often have to drill holes into wooden stands, however, to accommodate tank plumbing. These holes often expose the basic wood product and allow water to enter during a spill. Generally, a single spill will not cause a problem. If a slow leak develops, however, the water can find its way into the material comprising the load-bearing parts of the stand. This water influx can cause swelling and loss of strength. Although this ultimately could cause the stand to collapse, I have never actually heard of this happening. I have, however, known hobbyists who, upon discovering significantly swelling patches on the side of their stands due to unnoticed, slow-drip leaks, rapidly replaced their system's stands. Wood byproduct stands generally are more expensive than metal stands and have a completely enclosed storage and work space.

WOODEN STANDS

Often the most expensive stands are those made of wood. They often are made of oak or another hardwood, and they generally are attractive pieces of furniture. Wooden stands are strong and won't be affected by leaks. They also completely enclose the work space under the tank. For many people, they are the stand of choice. They might cost more, however, than most of the other system components put together.

HOMEMADE STANDS

Many hobbyists, even beginners, make their own stands. If you are gifted with woodworking abilities, this is not terribly difficult. Strong, attractive and serviceable stands can be made relatively inexpensively. If you go this route, however, remember that it is probably prudent to over-engineer your stand so it will support significantly more than just the weight of your tank. This provides a safety factor that can help avert catastrophe. Custom-built stands often can provide much in the way of extra amenities if the hobbyist is sure of what he wants to put in the stand. Extra shelving for equipment or storage, for example, can be installed from the beginning, as can a small lighting system for ease of servicing pumps and equipment.

The Sump

Sumps are additional reservoirs of system water placed somewhere in the system's water circuit. The basic plumbing scheme of most reef systems connects the main tank to a sump, often by an overflow pipe out of the main tank down to the sump hidden in the stand. Water is moved back up to the aquarium by a large pump either submerged into or connected to the sump. This circuit provides the basic water movement in the system.

USES FOR A SUMP

This water movement can be accomplished without a sump, so why go to the extra trouble of installing one? There are several reasons to have a sump. A sump increases the amount of water volume for the system and makes the system more stable. Other somewhat unsightly equipment, such as heaters, can be placed in the sump and out of the tank. In addition, kalkwasser equipment can be placed in the sump; this allows the dilution of the additive before it gets into the main tank. A sump can hold filters and protein skimmers, and it can be the place of water replacement and drainage during water changes. This avoids stressing some of the animals in the main tank. Finally, a sump or portions of it can be converted into a refugium, a subsidiary sand bed.

> ### GET READY FOR SOME NOISE
>
> For a 100-gallon tank, a waterfall coming out of the back of the tank flushes 30 gallons a minute from the main tank to the sump. This is the equivalent of a full bathtub draining every minute into the sump—every minute of every hour of every day all year. Because this process involves lots of turbulent water, it is *not* silent. Many things can be done to minimize the noise, but the noise will always be there. There also is the noise of the pump itself. Although pumps are not exceptionally noisy, they do produce noticeable sound. The moral of this tale is that the aquarium can seriously interfere with listening to a stereo or the television. For the health of the animals, however, you cannot just turn it off.

SUMP SIZE

There's no hard and fast rule for the size of the sump. Generally, most experienced aquarists feel it is best to set up the largest sump the stand can accommodate, and this is the practice I recommend to the beginner. I know of systems in which the display aquarium is about 50 gallons, but the sump is more than 500 gallons. On the other hand, I also know of and maintain systems with no sump whatsoever. Plan ahead here! The sump also will contain a significant amount of water and, once set up, will be immobile. Most stands are designed to support weight on top where the main tank is. They might not be able to support much weight on the lower shelf, so the hobbyist might have to add support to this shelf to accommodate the sump.

A sump increases the amount of water for the system, rendering it more stable. A stable system is one in which the animals thrive.

SUMP MATERIALS

Unless a refugium is built into it, the sump is designed as a working area and is not a place for animals to live. Consequently, there's no need for the sump to be built from the same materials as the main aquarium. In fact, there are many reasons to use an entirely different type of material. Many aquarists use large plastic or rubber containers for the sumps. They are sturdy, don't break and can be drilled to accommodate pumps and plumbing. Additionally, you can use hot melted glue and thin pieces of acrylic or other plastics to subdivide the sump to make maintenance more efficient. As with the actual system, the sump can be very simple or very complex and is dependent on the hobbyist's needs.

REFUGIA

A refugium is an area in the plumbing circuit of the tank that contains an isolated area of biological substrate. This often is a secondary sand bed with some algae, and illumination usually is provided. The purpose of the refugium is to provide an area in which the small organisms and microorganisms of the sand bed and algae can exist and thrive without the potential threat of predation by the larger animals of the main aquarium. Recent evidence indicates that small microorganisms and small crustaceans, in particular, are important foods for many of the tank's inhabitants. The fish and larger invertebrates, however, often have the capability to reduce the populations of these animals in the main tank to a level in which self-replenishing populations cannot exist.

Because the refugium is in the main water circuit and is not isolated from the tank in any way, as the animals inside reach high populations and start to swim around, they are swept with the water flow into the main tank. Here they can persist, but they also can be eaten, providing a continual food source for many of the filter-feeding corals, soft corals and other animals in the main tank. For appropriate functioning of the refugium, sufficient water flow must pass over it. It should not be isolated in any way from the main tank circulation pattern except to exclude the large animals.

The refugium can simply consist of a container, such as a small wash basin, of tank sediment in the sump. More elaborate arrangements are possible and are limited only by the aquarist's imagination, pocketbook and desire. The entire floor to the sump often is converted into a second sand bed filter such as might be found in the main tank. Additionally, you can provide sufficient lighting for algal growth in the system and can use the refugium as a place to grow algae to harvest.

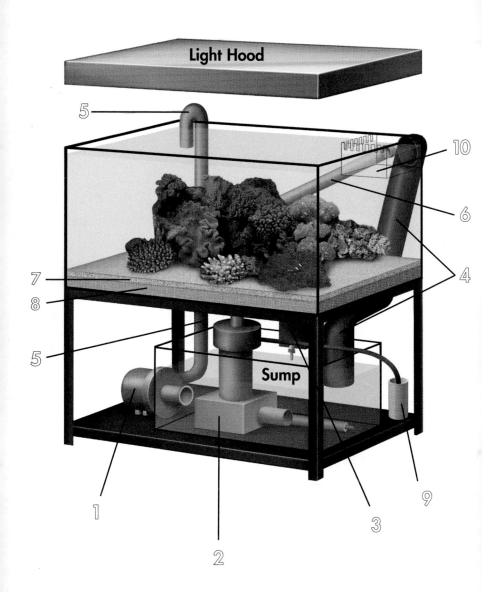

Light Hood

Sump

This diagram shows one of many possible arrangements for a coral reef aquarium. The sides of the stand are not shown so that the equipment layout may be illustrated. Electrical cords have not been drawn to avoid unnecessary clutter. No power-heads have been shown in the tank, but they may be placed wherever desired. The main tank is assumed to have been drilled to allow for water movement.

1) Main circulation pump—draws water from the sump through a bulkhead fitting and sends it to the tank through the tank inlet pipe (#5).

2) Protein skimmer (in the sump)—receives water from a separate pipe (#6) from the overflow box (#10).

3) Limewater (Kalkwasser)—drip container fastened to the top of the stand. Fluid drips into the sump through an adjustable valve.

4) Main tank overflow pipe—receives water from the overflow box through a bulkhead fitting.

5) Tank inlet pipe—takes water from the pump and conveys it to the tank.

6) Skimmer inlet pipe—takes water to the skimmer from the overflow box.

7) Upper layer of oxygenated gravel.

8) Lower layer of gravel—with reduced oxygen concentration.

9) Skimmer waste collection container.

10) Overflow box.

These algae provide both habitat and food for many of the microorganisms supported by the refugia. Their growth can do the double duty of removing excess nutrients and providing food for the system.

Water Pump and Basic Plumbing

The main aquarium and sump/refugium are connected by the system's plumbing, and water is moved through that system by the main circulation pump. Without adequate water circulation, you will not be able to maintain the animals that make the reef a reef. Water must flow through the main tank relatively rapidly and be exchanged frequently. It is almost impossible to have too much water flow, at least with regard to the animals. As with all things, however, compromises must be made.

Sump, pump and tank—one easy way to plumb the connection of the tank to the pump is with a bulkhead fitting through a hole in the wall of the sump.

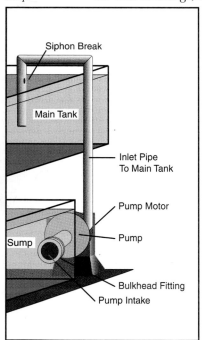

Siphon Break

Main Tank

Inlet Pipe
To Main Tank

Pump Motor

Pump

Sump

Bulkhead Fitting

Pump Intake

High water flow means large pumps, which in turn draw a lot of electric current. These pumps must remain on continuously, and the electrical cost over the course of a year can be considerable. All mechanical equipment eventually fails, and an emergency back-up should be available. Moreover, a lot of water flow can mean a lot of noise. The water in a reef aquarium should be completely exchanged at least 10 times an hour as an absolute minimum. Thus, for a 100-gallon aquarium, the main circulation pump should be capable of moving a thousand or more gallons an hour.

Typically, water leaves the main tank through an overflow box or bulkhead fittings. Many acrylic tanks come with these built in. Others are available for purchase to fit to glass tanks. These are designed to allow the water to leave the tank, but they have a barrier to prevent the animals in the tank from being sucked out of the system. The water flows through rigid pipes or flexible tubing to the sump. The sump typically has a bulkhead fitting built into one end, and a pipe or tube connects to the main pump, which then pushes water back up to the tank.

Waterfall sounds can be minimized by reducing turbulent splashing or gurgling. These sounds are generated by water being forced through pipes rather than flowing smoothly. Smooth flow can be facilitated by using larger pipes and by matching flow to the pipe to prevent the sucking of air into the system. To a large extent, obtaining a smooth flow is accomplished by trial and error. Valves can be put in the pipes at any point during the construction of the system to regulate flow, and it is better to put them in and not need them than to need them and not have them. The water should enter the sump below the sump's water level. This minimizes splashing sounds and eliminates a lot of mess.

> ### GET THE WATER TEMPERATURE RIGHT AT THE START
>
> A word to the wise: Do temperature calibration and setting *before* you add your expensive livestock! Poached sea anemones smell *really* awful!

The waterfall sounds also will diminish after a week or two as the insides of the pipes and tubing become covered with a thin biofilm layer that significantly reduces noise. Generally, the noises will drop off to a tolerable level after the system is adjusted a bit. At a certain point, the noise of the system tends to become white noise, which can easily be ignored.

Bulkhead fittings to connect tanks or sumps to pipes or tubing are available in many reef aquarium stores, mail-order pet-supply stores or hardware stores. They generally consist of Polyvinyl Chloride (PVC) fittings and a gasket. Follow the instructions that come with them to avoid leakage. The plumbing of the reef tank can be easily accomplished and is inexpensive. Generally, the aquarist can use Schedule 40 PVC pipe, which is available from most hardware stores. The pipe can be connected using special glues. If you are not familiar with gluing PVC, ask a hardware-store attendant for some brief instructions. Cutting and gluing PVC pipe is an easy process, but once glued, the joints cannot be unglued. It pays to be careful and to do it right the first time. The old carpenter's adage of "measure twice, cut once" is very relevant here. There also are screw fittings made for PVC, and they often are useful. Remember that, when you mate the two parts of the screw fitting, you need to cover the threads with Teflon (TFE) tape to prevent leakage.

Flexible PVC tubing also is available, often at spa and hot-tub stores. Installing flexible tubing helps dampen out excess vibrations. Some hardware stores carry transparent vinyl tubing that can be useful to connect various components, but be sure to get the tubing reinforced with PVC threads. Without the reinforcement, the tubing will eventually split. Speaking from experience, it is an awesome sight to watch such a tube split lengthwise spraying 30 gallons of seawater onto your living room carpet each minute. You might be amazed at how fast you can move to shut off the system . . .

CONNECTION CONSIDERATIONS

When connecting all the parts of the system, put ballvalves and disconnect joints on both sides of any component you might want to remove and service such as pumps, skimmers and the sump. Also consider what might happen in the case of a plumbing failure. If the water is entering your tank through a pipe that is continuous without any holes in it, you have created a siphon. With any break in the system or power outage, the water will flow out of that siphon and will drain the tank to the level of the pipe's first opening. If the opening of the pipe is placed near the bottom of the tank, such a leak will drain the entire tank. The remedy for this is to drill a small hole in the inlet pipe just below the tank's normal water level. If there's a power outage or a break, the tank will only drain slightly. In a power outage, this prevents the tank from draining backwards into the sump, which would fill and overflow. In the case of a plumbing failure, the water in the line might drain, but the volume of water in the tank would be contained. Although your carpet might become trash, your livestock would not be harmed.

THE MAIN PUMP

Proper functioning of the main pump is crucial. This pump not only must be able to move water, it must pump it up from the sump to the tank. This upward distance is called the head of pressure. The back pressure on most aquarium water pumps is significant, and the flow loss over a 4- or 5-foot rise can be as much as 50 percent of the flow. Such a pump, although rated at a flow rate of 1000 gallons an hour, would only move about 500 gallons per hour through your tank. There are a considerable number of water pumps on the market, and it pays to shop around and purchase one with as much extra capacity as you can afford.

These pumps are all electrically driven centrifugal pumps. Most run off household current, but they can draw enough amperage to warrant minimizing the other uses of that circuit. Plan ahead for potential leaks or disasters and mount any electrical connections that have to be made either outside the stand or in waterproof junction boxes (available at hardware stores).

If you have a flood in your stand (yes, we all have them— occasionally), *do not* reach into spraying salt water to pull electrical plugs to shut off the pump. Shut off the pump from a circuit breaker or a shut-off switch you have thoughtfully connected on the outside of your stand. Salt water conducts electricity very well, and you can electrocute yourself by mixing salt water and hot electrical lines. For safety's sake, install ground fault interrupter circuits on all electric outlets that might come in contact with salt water. These can easily be installed by either a hobbyist or an electrician, and they are available at local hardware stores.

Pumps produce both noise and heat. The noise can be dampened considerably by enclosing the pump in a small sound-proofing box constructed of Styrofoam insulation board. Simply cut the board as you would cut wood and fasten it together with nails or another fastener. Give the pump plenty of room so air can circulate in and around it. Most of the pump's heat is lost through the impeller shaft into your tank water. The amount of heat transmitted into the tank in this way can be considerable, depending on the pump.

Pumps need to be cleaned or serviced periodically. Plan on doing this! Put disconnect joints on both sides of the pump and position ball-valves to shut off the water flow close to the pump to minimize leakage. Be sure to place towels or containers under the disconnect joints to contain the leakage.

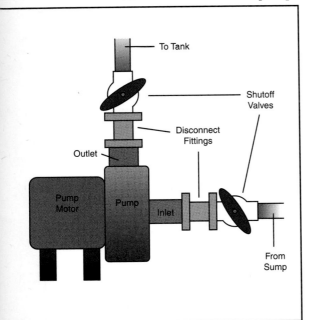

Main pump and valves—the main circulation pump should be plumbed so it can easily be removed and serviced. Disconnect fittings (PVC pipe junctions) and shut-off valves (PVC ball valves) should be connected to the pipes running to and from the tank.

Look for Leaks

After you have the system set up and plumbed, fill it with fresh water and turn on the pump. Inspect it carefully and find the leaks. If you can't find any leaks, you haven't looked closely enough. If after a thorough search you still don't find any leaks, buy as many lottery tickets as you can afford—you are decidedly lucky today. Mark the leaks with a grease pencil or another waterproof marker and drain the system. It is almost impossible to fix leaks with water in the system. Dry off the system in the area of the leak. If the leak is coming from a PVC pipe-glued joint, you should be able seal it by using a pipette to force glue or solvent into the joint in the area of the leak. After you do that, let it dry overnight and seal the joint with silicone aquarium sealant. You can use ordinary caulk instead of sealant only if it doesn't contain any chemicals to kill mildew and mold. Such chemicals can leak into the tank through contact with water and can be lethal to some organisms. Leaks in screw fittings often can be repaired by replacing the TFE tape over the threads.

POWERHEADS

When the tank is set up and running and you have introduced your livestock and decorations, you'll find you have areas of weak current or other places you want to increase or redirect the flow. These adjustments often are done with small submersible pumps called powerheads.

Powerheads are available in a wide variety of shapes and sizes. Many have features that will never be utilized; others have features you can't live without. Determination of the right features often is a matter of personal taste. If very strong extra currents are needed in the system, some pumps can be mounted outside the tank with their impellers and outlets inside the tank.

Powerheads are almost a necessity for most reef systems; however, they have one major drawback. They are ugly as sin, and most aquarists take great pains to camouflage them, often to the point of burying them in the decorative rock. This is not the right thing to do, and it becomes evident when the pump needs to be cleaned or serviced. Powerheads should be mounted in an easily accessible place. All powerheads and pump inlets also need to be covered with a grating, mesh or screen to prevent animals from being sucked into them. Most marine animals have no natural experience with point-source sucking currents and have no natural avoidance responses. Putting the screen on saves the lives of your animals, prevents fouling of the tank from the slurry made of dead animals killed by the pumps, and can save an expensive pump from impeller damage. These protective screens need to be cleaned frequently, often once a week or so. It is advisable to draw up a regular maintenance schedule that includes this task.

Filters for Mechanical Filtration

The removal of materials from the water by strictly mechanical filtration (as opposed to the removal by biological filtration) is a process that is critical for the maintenance of your aquarium. This process, however, must be done carefully to avoid removing essential materials from the system. There are a number of different types of filtration, but the most important are called protein skimmers.

PROTEIN SKIMMERS—FOAM FRACTIONATERS

Foam fractionation, better known by the incorrect title of protein skimming, is a process that takes place in natural waters and causes sea foam. It also is a process that aquarists can accentuate to provide a way to export numerous undesirable materials from the system.

Aquarium animals, particularly fish, excrete phosphate into the water. Protein skimmers create and collect "sea foam" containing phosphate, keeping the water clean.

Foam fractionation works because a lot of large organic molecules and other materials tend to collect on a water-air interface. If many small bubbles are forced into a column of water, the amount of air-water interface is immense. These bubbles will collect a lot of undesirable chemicals on their surfaces. If the bubbles are allowed to rise in a column, they coalesce and burst resulting in foam. The surface of that foam is rich in excess organic nutrients and some other materials such as phosphates. If the foam is collected and removed, the materials are exported from the system. Protein skimming coupled with good biological filtration is all the filtration most tanks need on a regular basis. Any other filtration should be considered supplemental, to be used only occasionally or on an emergency basis.

Generally, skimmers require a dedicated pump to move water through them. They often are placed in the sump drawing from and discharging to the sump. If the inlet and outflow tubes are placed correctly, the potential problem of reskimming the same water is minimized. The water pump driving the skimmer moves water through a column from top to bottom; the bubbles move in the other direction counter to the flow of the water.

This countercurrent exchange mechanism results in the maximum filtration. Because of the number of the bubbles and the length of time they are in the water column, gas exchange also is facilitated across the bubble membranes. The water exiting a good foam fractionator is fully aerated, and there is no need for any additional aeration such as air stones, bubble bars or air pumps.

SELECTING A SKIMMER

A few good designs of protein skimmers work well and can provide reasonable skimming. There are two things to keep in mind when purchasing a protein skimmer. First, skimming success depends on the number and size of the bubbles. The more small bubbles produced, the better the skimmer. Second, the longer these bubbles are in contact with the water column, the better the skimmer. In general, this means small skimmers are not acceptable for any but the smallest systems.

There are basically three types of protein skimmers. The first are air-driven skimmers in which the bubbles are created by an air pump. In the best of these, the air is pumped through pieces of basswood, which sometimes also is called limewood. This creates a tremendous quantity of very fine bubbles. These skimmers can be very effective, particularly if the countercurrent water column is long. In some commercial bubble skimmers, the column might be eight or more feet long. A significant drawback to these skimmers is the need to replace the wooden bubble generators when the blocks clog or start to produce large bubbles. Generally, the blocks don't last much beyond a month or so, and they often need to be replaced far more frequently.

The second type of skimmer uses a venturi to create the bubble flow. These skimmers typically require a large and powerful water pump to work well, but they can be more efficient than air-driven skimmers. They also don't need the subsidiary air pump or the basswood blocks. They too work best with a very long column.

The third type of skimmer is referred to as a down-draft skimmer because it uses a powerful pump to force

*Down-draft foam
fractionator—the
amount of skim-
mate collected by
these devices can
be substantial,
and the collec-
tion cup should
be connected to a
bucket to receive
excess waste.*

water mixed with air down through a column filled with materials to cause the water spray to be broken up. Air is sucked into the water stream at the top of the column. At the bottom of the column, the cascading foam stream is contained in a box designed to retard the water flow through it. A second column is placed downstream of the first, and foam rises in this column to be collected at the top. Down-draft skimmers have another distinct advantage—if the kalkwasser drip line is inserted in the air injector, the kalkwasser causes a significantly increased removal of phosphate. This is caused by the precipitation of particulate calcium phosphate in the down-draft tube where it can be periodically removed during skimmer maintenance. The removal of phosphate in this system can be several hundred times more efficient than with any other methods.

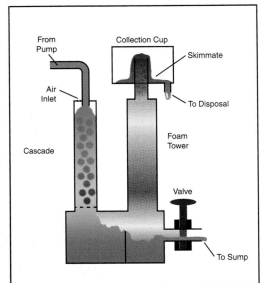

Long collection columns for all three types of skimmers will maximize the removal of the undesirable materials. The down-draft skimmer, however, with two columns and a foam box at the bottom can do the same amount of filtration in significantly less space than a correspondingly effective skimmer of the other designs.

The size of the stand often limits the size of the skimmer that can be placed in it, and this tends to favor down-draft skimmers over the other models. Unfortunately, down-draft skimmers are significantly more complex and more expensive than the other types of skimmers. A trade-off between cost and efficiency is imposed on aquarists here.

All these skimmers collect their effluent or skimmate in a collection vessel at the top of the column. All skimmers can be adjusted to allow the skimmate to be very dry or quite wet. Dry skimmate contains organic materials and little water. Wet skimmate can contain trace elements and other materials that the aquarist might want to keep in the aquarium. After the material is collected in the vessel at the top of the column, it can be discarded. In some skimmers, there is the possibility to have a drain tube connecting the collection vessel with a bucket, jar or some other easily removable container to discard the skimmate.

All skimmers need to be cleaned periodically to remove the bacterial film that collects on the inside of the collection vessel or column. This material can become quite thick and foul-smelling, and it looks like mud. The removal of this material should be done on a regular basis. Consequently, the skimmer must be positioned in the sump or somewhere else that allows easy access. All the different skimmers might need to be entirely removed from the sump when being cleaned.

PARTICULATE FILTRATION

Regular filtration to remove small particles is neither necessary nor desirable in a reef tank set up as an artificial ecosystem. The sand bed will be producing plankton that acts as food for many of the suspension-feeding animals in the system. Additionally, the sand fauna maintains itself by regular reproduction, and the larvae are found in the water of the system. This type of mechanical filtration removes the larvae and the microplanktonic food. Occasional particulate filtration might be necessary from time-to-time to clear up cloudiness or if there are undesirable particulates in water. In these cases, a filter can be used for short periods of three to four days.

Chemical Filtration

After some length of time—the period will vary with the tank and its inhabitants—the water will become decidedly yellow. This is due to the accumulation of humic acids. These are rather unsightly and can significantly interfere with light transmission. They can be removed with filtration utilizing Granulated Activated Carbon (GAC). I find that the easiest way to do this is to use a filter in the sump instead of a filter medium. GAC is put into the filter compartment in a fine mesh bag. The carbon should be of high quality and lacking in phosphate, and it should be rinsed well prior to its use in the aquarium. After the filter has been working for several days, the water should be noticeably less colored.

During this period, a significant amount of light-absorbing pigment is removed from the water, and it might be best to lower light intensity or duration to about 80 percent of the preceding period. Be aware that the increased radiation suddenly available after the carbon filtration can seriously burn some sensitive animals. After the filter is removed, the light intensity should gradually come back to normal over several days.

Lights

Some of the more colorful giant clams do well in home mini-reefs, even though in nature they live under much greater light intensity.

Shallow-water tropical sunlight is very intense, typically far more intense than we can duplicate in our homes without considerable effort and expense. Indeed, equatorial light is so intense that very few marine animals can withstand it without some sort of protection. A much smaller number of animals can live in the shallow-water tropics than in slightly deeper localities; however, these animals include some of the brighter-color varieties of corals and giant clams. Fortunately for the novice hobbyist, they often thrive at the lower light intensities available for use in the home.

Light is both absorbed and scattered upon entering water, and the inverse square law governs light intensity. This relationship dictates that the light intensity 2 feet from a light source has ¼ the intensity of the light one foot from the source. This means that light intensity in our tanks drops off quite dramatically. If the tank is 2 feet deep and the light is placed one foot above the surface water layer, the light intensity halfway though the tank is $\frac{1}{4}$ the intensity at the surface. At the bottom, the intensity is $\frac{1}{9}$ the surface intensity. This means that animals requiring high light intensities must be placed in shallow positions in our systems.

Various methods of providing light to the reef tank have been used, including standard incandescent bulbs, normal output fluorescent bulbs (NO bulbs), very high output fluorescent bulbs (VHO bulbs), power compact fluorescent bulbs (PC bulbs) and metal halide bulbs (MH bulbs). Only the last two types are consistently successful at maintaining most of the animals reef aquarists want to keep.

Much has been written, and undoubtedly will continue to be written, about illumination in general, light intensity, light spectral differences and the needs of photosynthetic organisms in reef aquariums. Much of this is nonsense. As long as the light is sufficiently bright to saturate the chlorophyll in the zooxanthellae or algae, sufficient photosynthetic product will be produced to facilitate growth. Remarkably few useable data from natural coral reefs can be applied directly to our artificial ecosystems. Basically, the organisms need light that has sufficient intensity in the peak bluish and reddish spectral regions so photosynthesis can proceed at a normal rate. This can be accomplished easily with the appropriate MH and PC bulbs. It is hard to do with VHO bulbs, however, and it is impossible to do with NO and incandescent bulbs.

METAL HALIDE BULBS

The most popular of the acceptable lighting methods is illumination by metal halide bulbs. Metal halides are highly modified incandescent bulbs that provide a point source of very bright light. Such light provides a pleasing ripple effect on the aquarium surface.

Additionally and more importantly, metal halide lights provide illumination intense enough to saturate the photosynthetic capability of the zooxanthellae in their various hosts, thereby providing adequate nutrition from these sources. A wide variety both of sizes and colors of metal halide bulbs are available. The power of the basic bulbs starts at 175 watts and goes upward. For a tank of less than 50 gallons, generally a single 175-watt bulb is sufficient; for tanks between 50 and 100 gallons, two bulbs often are used. Larger tanks can use either larger bulbs, more bulbs or both.

The bulbs also are classified by color temperature measured in degrees Kelvin. The most inexpensive bulbs typically have a color rendition of 5500 degrees Kelvin and give a slightly yellowish light. Bulbs with color renditions of 6500 degrees and higher are progressively more bluish. The 5500-degree Kelvin bulbs produce sufficient and adequate light for the aquarium inhabitants, but the other bulbs often give a light more pleasing to the aquarist. The bulbs with higher Kelvin temperatures are significantly more expensive, and they also need to be replaced more frequently.

Keep in mind that all lights generate heat and that corals cannot withstand prolonged periods of great heat. A small fan will help mitigate the heating effect of your lights.

All metal halides change color and lose intensity as they are used. Most authorities recommend replacing the bulbs about every six months. I've found, however, that my bulbs seem to be adequate for longer periods, and I replace mine about every nine months to a year. To compensate for the slightly yellowish color of the inexpensive bulbs, many hobbyists use a duplex light fixture containing the metal halide bulb and one or more bluish "actinic" fluorescent bulbs. These fixtures produce light both pleasing to the eye and adequate for all the organisms likely to be maintained by a beginning hobbyist. Very importantly, they also are significantly more cost effective than using only higher color-temperature metal halide bulbs.

All lighting sources, but particularly metal halide lights, produce significant heat and can raise the temperature of the tanks considerably, in some cases enough to cause lethal effects. To accelerate evaporation and to cool the tank, place a small fan so it blows across the surface of the water.

Metal halide lights also can provide a good deal of ultraviolet illumination. This mimics nature to some extent, and it might be responsible for some the bright pigments found in shallow-water corals. These pigments are thought to be a protective mechanism preventing the lethal effects of ultraviolet radiation. Most metal halide light fixtures come with UV shields that absorb much of this high-energy light. These shields can be removed if the hobbyist desires; whether this increases the brightness of the coral colors is still open to debate. Note that removal of the UV shields can lead to burns, exercise caution and never look directly at an unshielded bulb.

POWER COMPACT FLUORESCENT BULBS

Recently, power compact fluorescent bulbs have been marketed toward the reef hobby. As with metal halide lighting, several different color temperatures and sizes are available. The bulbs have several advantages over the MH lighting. First, they run cooler, eliminating some of the worries about overheating. Second, the bulbs last much longer—12 to 24 months as opposed to the 6 months or so recommended for metal halide bulbs. Finally, the average bulb costs far less initially and is of lower wattage, so it costs less to operate as well.

Power compact fluorescent bulbs also have some disadvantages. Because the lights are not point source illuminators, they do not create the ripple effect that many people find especially pleasing. In addition, they produce less intense light and less UV illumination, which some believe is a cause of bright coral colors, than the metal halide bulbs. Notably, more bulbs must be utilized to obtain a similar level of total illumination. This is easily done, however. All corals can be adequately grown under both metal halide and power compact bulbs. It is up to you to determine whether the extra costs of the metal halide bulbs provide sufficient extra benefit.

NORMAL OUTPUT AND VERY HIGH OUTPUT FLUORESCENT BULBS

Both normal output and very high output fluorescent bulbs produce significantly less illumination than the metal halide and power compact bulbs. They can, however, be mounted more closely to increase the amount of light available from a given fixture. By themselves, they cannot provide sufficient illumination to support most zooxanthellae-bearing animals, but they can illuminate tanks sufficiently to maintain low light–tolerant corals and non-zooxanthellate–bearing animals. They should not be used, however, as the sole source of illumination for most shallow-water corals or giant clams.

Both normal output and very high output bulbs are available in a variety of colors and sizes. Only the highest intensity bulbs are suitable for reef aquarium illumination. These bulbs frequently are used as subsidiary lighting in fixtures containing metal halide bulbs. Some hobbyists use them to simulate the lower light intensities found around dawn and dusk. Actinic fluorescent bulbs also can be used to add blue light to balance the slight yellowish cast of 5500-watt metal halide bulbs.

INCANDESCENT BULBS

Standard incandescent bulbs have no purpose in the general illumination of coral reef aquariums. Their light is too feeble, and it is far too yellow.

Reef Temperature

Coral reef aquariums need to be maintained at the temperatures of normal coral reefs. These temperatures vary somewhat from region to region. All of the most diverse coral reefs have temperatures that fluctuate from about 82°F to about 87°F and that average around 84°F. As the temperature decreases away from the equator, the reefs get cooler and the number of coral species decreases as well.

Reef corals generally cannot survive in temperatures below 68°F. Most corals are found in areas where the water temperature never gets below 80°F. Although they can tolerate cooler water, most do not grow well at these temperatures. Numerous scientific studies have shown that coral grows most rapidly in water temperatures ranging from 82°F to 84°F. All coral reef algae and animals thrive at temperatures in that range, and it is ideal for the home aquarium.

Corals and other reef animals begin to suffer the effects of overheating during periods of prolonged temperatures above about 90°F. Occasional hot days in the summer are well tolerated, but periods of several

Corals, algae and fish all thrive at temperatures in the 82°F to 84°F range.

days at or above 90°F likely will cause problems. These problems can include ejection of zooxanthellae (bleaching), abnormal behavior and even death. Reefs maintained at temperatures around 84°F are somewhat accommodated to and more resistant to high-temperature effects.

How to Control the Temperature

Optimum temperatures can easily be maintained by any number of heating system types. Most inexpensive submersible heaters are quite reliable. Once properly set, they can maintain the temperature above a minimum without any further work on your part. Many of these heaters have an internal indicator of temperature to allow for easy adjusting. These indicators should not be considered too accurate. Adjust the heat to approximately the right range and allow the temperature of the system to come to equilibrium. Check the temperature with a good thermometer and adjust the heater up or down accordingly. Remember,

Submersible heaters are a good way to maintain the necessary temperature of a system. As a general rule, your heater should have about 5 watts of heating capacity for each gallon of system capacity. (Don't forget the sump!)

it might take several hours for the aquarium to reach the equilibrium temperature.

If you live in a consistently warm area and you cannot maintain your dwelling temperature below the low 90s, you might want to invest in a chiller to set an upper limit on the temperature your system can reach. There are many chillers on the market, and most work sufficiently well. Remember to test the chiller before you have to rely on it to save your ecosystem from heat death. After installing the chiller, either increase the temperature of your room above the threshold value or put an extra heater or two in the sump and attempt to increase the temperature of the system. Verify that the unit can keep the temperature within acceptable ranges.

Most aquarists have absolutely no need for chillers. Small fans and evaporative cooling can maintain temperature levels very well for most systems. If it appears that the temperature will spike well over 90°F in the system, turn off one or more of the lights for the day or even for several days. It gets dim in the tropics on occasion, and a day or two of reduced light intensity will not harm any of the aquarium denizens and will significantly lower the temperature in the tank.

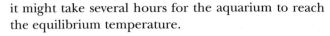

Submersible Heater

Temperature Adjustment

Electric Cord

Temperature Indicator

-82-

Indicator Light

Heater Element

Glass Tube

Chemical Testing Equipment

Part of maintaining the appropriate water chemistry is the necessity, at least initially, to monitor and maintain chemical levels. To this end, I recommend purchasing and using several chemical test kits. The novice hobbyist should keep a log of tests including dates, test runs and results and, most importantly, the appearance of the animals. Eventually, you will be able to detect changes in water parameters simply by carefully observing the livestock. When this skill is acquired, you might want to decrease the frequency of water testing.

These are basic conditions that need to be tested: pH, calcium levels, alkalinity, phosphate concentration, ammonia concentration, nitrite concentration, nitrate concentration, copper concentration and iodine concentration.

As a rule, testing for ammonia and nitrite only needs to be done after the initial setup of the system. There should be noticeable values of these chemicals only until the biological filter is established. After that point, the chemicals should be undetectable. Use tests after that point to verify correct functioning of the sand bed filter. Also test if a problem suddenly appears that has system-wide effects indicating that perhaps a large animal has died or that something has happened to the filter.

Except for copper, these chemicals need to be tested regularly, and the system should be adjusted as necessary. Low calcium readings, for example, indicate that *kalkwasser* or

> ### AVOID COMMERCIAL CLEANERS FOR THE HOME
>
> Soap and other cleaning materials should never be used in marine systems. Many of these materials are designed to cut through grease, and they do an equally good job of cutting though the cell membranes of (and killing) many marine animals. Care must also be taken when cleaning the outside of the tank. Many glass cleaners contain significant amounts of ammonia, and aerosol applicators deposit much of this material into the air. Cleaning the glass of the tank with a pump aerosol spray of ammonia cleaner is a good way to support your local fish store with the purchase of replacement animals.

some other calcium supplement should be added and that alkalinity should be tested to verify that it also is within acceptable ranges. Increasing levels of nitrate indicate that a feeding-rate adjustment might be necessary, along with the need to encourage some macroalgal growth so nutrients can be exported. Tests should be done regularly and trends should be noted. Trends are more important than spot readings because considerable fluctuations occur from time to time that have absolutely no long-term significance. It seems to be an enduring myth that the natural coral reef environment is a stable one. This is true only if the stability is considered to be about average values; the fluctuations around the average often can be quite considerable even on a daily basis. Small fluctuations in values are to be expected without concern. Large fluctuations and progressive trends are stronger indicators of problems.

Copper needs to be tested in the water used to mix salt water. If this water contains any copper, a copper-removal treatment must be performed before each batch of water is mixed. Copper is lethal to many marine invertebrate at exceptionally low doses. Copper should never be

added to a marine aquarium, and in general, any material that has had copper in it is not suitable for a marine aquarium.

Bells and Whistles

The coral reef aquarium hobby is one that lends itself to technology, and

Ultimately, your organisms are the best testing devices in your tank. Observe your aquarium and learn to recognize the signs of health in your animals.

many techno-groovy toys are available for the hobbyist. Many of them are useful, but many are most useful at separating the hobbyist's cash from the hobbyist's bank account. I have tried throughout this book to indicate inexpensive and reliable methodology. If you, as the hobbyist, feel you need a certain piece of equipment to maintain your system, by all means support the manufacturer and purchase it. Try not to lose sight, however, that the goal of the hobby is a well-run aquarium system with healthy animals and that this can be done with a minimum of equipment and expense.

The best testing devices you have are the organisms in your system. Once you know what they look like when healthy and in good condition, it is easy to determine when a factor has changed for the worse. A few simple tests often can determine what has changed and can point to an easy course of remedial action. Instead of spending time examining new equipment, hobbyists should study their systems and their organisms to learn their characteristics and to learn how they change in various conditions. This knowledge can be obtained only through observation and manipulation of the system. It is easy to delegate running the system to various pieces of machinery but it is wiser to learn how to identify a problem on your own.

chapter 5

Your Reef System

In the previous chapters, I've babbled on about the various ecological, physical and chemical processes occurring in a marine reef aquarium as well as the equipment needed for the system. In this chapter, I will discuss the physical environment of the artificial eco-system. Spending a little time, effort and money at the initial stages of aquarium construction to ensure the correct physical conditions can save a lot of  time and grief later. As I've detailed in previous chapters, the organisms take the raw physical environment you give them and modify it so it can easily support a beautiful and diverse biological array. You do, however, have to give them the right materials on which to work their magic.

The basic ingredient of the system, of course, is water. Getting the water to be acceptable for life often is the most difficult task hobbyists face. Reef aquarists have to pay particular attention to the source of their water and what is in it.

If natural sea-water is available to you, it is a great choice for your tank.

Natural Seawater

Hobbyists living in some coastal communities might find that they can purchase filtered ocean water from local commercial aquariums or educational facilities. If such water is available, it probably is the best source of water you can use. Natural seawater has a number of attributes unavailable in artificial seawater. Especially important are exceptionally minute amounts of various biologically active chemicals, most probably of bacterial origin, that seem to facilitate life. Aged aquarium water also seems to have these particular materials in it, but it seems to take a few weeks before the aquarium microorganisms are properly able to condition the water. If this source of water is available to you, by all means use it if you can. Check with your local aquarium stores or reef aquarium society to determine the availability. Coastal water might be lower in salinity than we need for our aquariums, but it's an easy matter to bring it up to the necessary level by adding small amounts of artificial salt mix.

Making Your Own

Most aquarists have to make artificial seawater using fresh water and a salt mix. There's a wide range of quality in both of these raw materials, and some are definitely better than others.

YOUR TAP WATER

Generally, most people's freshwater source is the tap in their house or apartment. Such water has been variously treated, filtered and contaminated. From the aspect of the reef hobbyist, most of what is done to water to make it suitable for human consumption has to be undone for the tank. Municipal or commercial water sources typically treat their water with toxic chemicals, generally chlorine or chloramine, to kill harmful microorganisms. These chemicals are present in small amounts in tap water and must be removed prior to use or they will poison many organisms you want to keep. The chemicals can be removed using dechlorinator solutions available at pet stores. Alternatively, the water used to mix the artificial reef water can be stored in a container open to the air and aerated or filtered for about 24 hours. This allows for the dissipation of these chemicals.

Beware of Copper

After municipal water leaves the treatment plant on its way to the hobbyist's home, it passes through pipes made of various materials, most of which do not leach detectable amounts of materials into the water. Once the water enters the pipes of the hobbyist's dwelling, however, problems can occur. Many water pipes in homes or apartment buildings are made of copper tubing soldered together with lead-based solder. Lead isn't too much of a problem for marine systems, but copper is exceptionally lethal to many marine organisms, even in the tiny amounts that can dissolve into the water as it stands in the pipes. It always is a good idea to let several gallons of water go down the drain prior to collecting your mixing water. Test your tap water with a

Crabs, like many marine organisms, simply cannot tolerate exposure to copper. Test your tap water and make sure to remove all copper before it goes in your tank.

copper test kit. If there are detectable levels, utilize one of the copper-removal chemicals that can be purchased from pet stores. Any detectable copper in reef water is too much.

Other Chemicals

Other factors also can influence the seawater. Many areas have hard water containing significant amounts of dissolved calcium and magnesium salts. Such water is perfectly acceptable as reef water, but the extra calcium might make it difficult to dissolve the salt mixture.

USING DISTILLED WATER

Some areas have water containing iron, sulfur or other dissolved materials. This water makes artificial salt water of dubious and uncertain quality. If you live in such an area, it probably is best either to not attempt reefkeeping or to mix your salt water from distilled or dionized water.

If used on a per-gallon basis for drinking, distilled or dionized water is relatively inexpensive. If used by the 30-gallon batch for mixing seawater, however, it can be prohibitively costly. In this case, the hobbyist might want to invest in a reverse osmosis/deionizing (RO/DI) system designed for the hobby. These systems use water pressure and special membranes to produce water without dissolved solids. Many systems are available that produce water of excellent quality at a reasonable cost.

Containers for Mixing

It should be a priority on your mixing agenda to select the right equipment. The water can be mixed in any container made of inert materials. Do not use metal buckets or any container that has been potentially contaminated with any solvent, metallic compound or soap.

In the long run, it pays to purchase and set aside mixing containers and utensils that will only be used in your aquarium. These materials must *never* be washed in soap or cleaning solvent. Soaps and solvents leave trace residues that can kill marine organisms in very small amounts. Two materials that can be used to clean any residues from mixing and aquarium vessels are clear white vinegar and household chlorine bleach. Dilute muriatic acid can be used in place of the vinegar but be very careful. This material is technical-grade hydrochloric acid and is *much* stronger than vinegar. It can remove both scale from your powerheads and skin from your hands with astounding rapidity. Nonetheless, it is an excellent solvent for hard-to-remove materials. All these materials can be rinsed off containers without leaving lethal traces. If you can detect an odor from cleaned containers, they are not clean enough. Residual bleach should be neutralized with dechlorinator. Use vinegar (acetic acid) to clean off mineral deposits and scale.

> ### AVOID WATER SOFTENERS
>
> When creating the water for your aquarium, do not use water from water softeners! Water softeners typically use ion-exchange resins to replace the ions in hard water with sodium and chloride (or table salt) ions, and they produce water with a low but noticeable quantity of salt in it. Using such water to mix artificial salt water can result in abnormal chemical balances and test readings.

The mixing container can be of any size and shape, but many aquarists use large plastic garbage cans that are purchased new and never used for any other purpose. These should be cleaned in fresh water and bleach, followed by a freshwater rinse. It generally is best to mix the seawater in large batches. The seawater mixes typically come in boxes, bags or buckets, and the contents can separate in mixing. By using all the materials in one container, you ensure a proper chemical balance when you are done. Mixed seawater can be stored indefinitely in a closed opaque container if you store, mix and aerate it thoroughly prior to use. If necessary, test the water's salinity or specific gravity as well.

The Right Salinity

Artificial seawater mixes typically list the amount of seawater they will make. These amounts are only approximate, and they generally are calculated based on making the seawater to a specific gravity value of 1.021, which is a salinity value of about 30 parts per thousand (ppt). The salinity in a reef tank must be higher than this.

The salinity of natural reef water varies from about 33 ppt to about 38 ppt. The best value for reef aquarium water is about 34 ppt to 35 ppt. Salinity must be monitored in both the mixing vessel and the aquarium. Salinity can be directly measured with electric salinity monitors; these generally are reasonably accurate but need to be recalibrated frequently. Alternatively, salinity can be indirectly measured by the use of hydrometers. Hydrometers

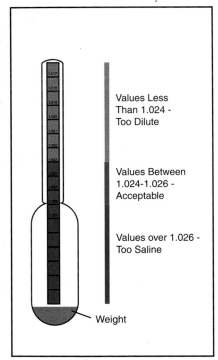

Values Less Than 1.024 - Too Dilute

Values Between 1.024-1.026 - Acceptable

Values over 1.026 - Too Saline

Weight

Floating glass hydrometers have a weight in the bottom, and the depth at which they float is calibrated to the internal scale.

measure the specific gravity of the water. The specific gravity is simply a number that tells how much a given volume of water will weigh compared to a volume of pure water. Pure water has a specific gravity close to 1.000 at 68°F (20°C); full-strength seawater at 35 ppt has a specific gravity of about 1.028 at that temperature. Acceptable and optimal values for the specific gravity and salinity are given in the following table. For the best health of your organisms, do not keep them for extended periods outside the values given in the table.

This table shows salinity in parts per thousand at the temperature and specific gravity indicated. Although all values in this table are acceptable, the optimum salinity values for organisms adapted to normal seawater are underlined. Sp. G. = Hydrometer value of specific gravity. These data were taken from values given in: Knudsen, M. (ed.) 1901. Hydrographical Tables. Williams & Northgate. London. 63 pp.

Specific Gravity	Temperature								
	80.0	**80.5**	**81.0**	**81.5**	**82.0**	**82.5**	**83.0**	**83.5**	**84.0**
1.023	33.2	33.3	33.4	33.5	33.6	33.7	33.8	33.9	34.0
1.024	34.5	34.6	34.7	34.8	34.9	35.0	35.2	35.3	35.4
1.025	35.8	35.9	36.0	36.1	36.3	36.4	36.5	36.6	36.7
1.026	37.1	37.3	37.4	37.5	37.6	37.7	37.8	37.9	38.1

Measuring Salinity

The type of hydrometer used to determine salinity is important. The most accurate and precise readings are given by large, immersible, glass hydrometers. These are expensive, however, are sometimes difficult to read and are fragile. Small, plastic, swing-arm hydrometers are available, but they sometimes give inaccurate readings, and they need to be calibrated against a glass hydrometer. Hydrometers need to be cleaned prior to use to ensure correct readings.

Adjusting Salinity

It is important to realize that marine organisms are adapted to a range of values for all factors such as temperature and salinity. Fluctuations within those ranges are easily tolerated and generally are of little consequence to the organism. Many organisms, however, respond with distress to rapid salinity changes, even though these changes are within normal ranges. Adjust salinity and acclimate animals to your tank's water slowly!

Water always evaporates from marine reef tanks; salt and dissolved minerals do not. After evaporation, the salinity of a system always will be higher than it was when the system was set up. Monitor the evaporation by testing salinity daily and by topping off the tank with either kalkwasser, dechlorinated tap water or RO/DI water.

Sediment

In addition to the water added to the tank, sediment needs to be added for the sand bed. It is best to add the sediment prior to the addition of any rocks, animals or water. If you use live sand as your substrate, however, the sediment has to be covered with seawater immediately after the sand is added.

SEDIMENT SIZE

Appropriate sediments are needed for the sand bed to maintain a diverse benthos. The sediment should contain particles of a wide variety of sizes and should not be uniform throughout. Particle diameters should range from coarse sand (2.0+ millimeters) to fine sand (0.063 millimeters). The sediments should be skewed so that about 60 percent of the sediment is between 0.5 millimeters and 0.062 millimeters in diameter (coarse sand to very fine sand), with the majority being about 0.125 millimeters in diameter. Sediment of this size often is advertised as "sugar-fine." This sediment-particle distribution facilitates water percolation and promotes organism utilization.

Finer particle sizes occur in the actual in-tank distribution because these sizes are the dust in dry sediments. Dust is effectively impossible to totally remove. Additionally, as the sediment organisms work and process sediments, small particles will develop from two sources. First, some of the sediment particles will be

eroded or partially dissolved making smaller sizes. Second, the fecal pellets deposited by the organisms living in the sediments and bacterial-detrital aggregations will form organic particles in the dust-size range. Both the inorganic and organic very fine particles will increase with time until they constitute a rather sizable percentage of the total sediments. This is not a cause for alarm, rather it is an indication that the bed is functioning properly. Eventually, an equilibrium between formation of these fine particles and their dissolution or reaggregation will be reached, and their relative contribution to the total sediment will stabilize.

Bristle worms and other bottom dwellers break up particles as they rustle about.

SEDIMENT COMPOSITION

As far as the animals are concerned, the mineral composition of the sediment is unimportant. Sediments composed of aragonitic particles, however, help maintain the calcium balance in the aquarium. Calcium carbonate can form several different minerals, although the

*Natural-colored
sands are safest
for your animals.*

most abundant ones are calcite and aragonite. Aragonite dissolves much more easily than calcite in seawater. A sediment bed made of aragonitic sand tends to dissolve when calcium levels are low in the tank and helps maintain calcium levels in an appropriate range.

Avoid utilizing river or masonry sand. Although very inexpensive, this sand generally is made of quartz, which is silica (SiO_2). Silica dissolves in minor amounts in seawater and fosters the growth of diatoms that can become very abundant as a brownish algal film growing on most everything.

Colored sands cause abnormal visual responses in some fish and invertebrates that have color vision. In some cases, the dyes used to give the color leach into the tank's water. It is best to keep away from colored sand.

Likewise, crushed coral is not an appropriate material for the sand bed except in small amounts. It is far too coarse in size and is useful only as a layer no more than ¼-inch thick on top of fine sediments. Such a layer serves to "armor" the fine sediments and prevents their dispersal by water currents in the tank.

Live Rock

There are two good reasons to add live rock to your reef aquarium. First, the bacteria in and on the porous rock significantly assist in the biological filtration. Second, live rock is highly decorative.

Depending on the source, live rock can be encrusted with all sorts of organisms. Both animals and algae can be found on it, and live rock typically is one of the sources to inoculate the tank with coralline algae, many small crustaceans (which serve both as part of the cleanup crew and as fish food) and worms. Some of the latter two also move into the sand bed and assist in maintaining its biodiversity.

MAKE SURE YOUR ROCK IS CURED

Live rock can be either cured or uncured. These terms reflect the amount of treatment the rock has had prior to its arrival in your home. When the rock is collected, it is covered with an immense growth of living organisms. Most of these organisms die during the shipping and handling process. Curing the rock is the process of allowing the rock to remain under water until all the material that is going to die does so and rots off the rock. The rock then undergoes a reestablishment of a mature bacteriological community. When this community is completely reestablished, the rock is considered cured.

The curing process results in the liberation of large amounts of nutrients, ammonia and nitrites. Such large amounts are released that the curing process can easily overwhelm even a well-established biological filter and can cause much secondary mortality in a system. Consequently, only cured rock is suitable for a beginning aquarium. Cured live rock often is available from reef aquarium stores or through mail-order outlets. Hobbyists can successfully cure their own rock, but such methodology is beyond the scope of this book.

SOURCES OF LIVE ROCK

There are many sources for natural live rock. The best live rock at any given moment can be determined by discussions with other hobbyists, particularly through computer online e-mail lists.

You might be able to get live rock from natural sources and aquaculture facilities. Rock from either source are likely to have comparable algal and bacterial diversity and abundance. The animal community on reef rock can take many years to become complete, however, and aquacultured rock typically is not grown for long enough to have a mature animal community on it. Consequently, it might be significantly less diverse than natural reef rock. On the other hand, much of this diversity dies when collected so this difference will probably count for little.

Natural reef rock from reputable collectors is reef rubble, and its collection is not at all deleterious to a reef. Aquacultured reef rock, however, made by using dead reef rock as a base, can be just as attractive as natural rock. Aquacultured reef rock made from concrete or cement does not work very well as a biological filter in the reef aquarium because it is insufficiently porous, although it might be very attractive. As might be expected, the rock varies widely in price depending on the source and shipping costs.

Ultimately, all the various types of rock are acceptable. Your choice should be based on your needs and your budget.

Chemical Additives

The final component of the environment is the materials added after the system is up and going. These are the various additives that can be put into the tank. Of these additives, the most important are those that help maintain the calcium and alkalinity balances. (These already have been discussed in the section on calcium metabolism, see Chapter 2.) Hobbyists must monitor and add calcium in some form, either as kalkwasser or as separate alkalinity and calcium supplements.

Almost all other additives to the reef system are unnecessary. The mythology that has built up around some of these additives is notable for its complete lack of *any* scientific data in support of them. Some absolutely unnecessary additives include strontium, magnesium and molybdenum, all of which can be poisonous to some animals in amounts only a little above the natural seawater concentrations. I strongly urge that these materials not be added to the aquarium. I realize, however, that some

CLEANERS FOR YOUR EQUIPMENT

You have to periodically clean powerheads and pumps or they eventually will fail. You can disassemble and soak them in vinegar to dissolve the scale that then can be rubbed off with a Teflon-coated scrubbing sponge. Use bleach to clean off organic slime, sludge or other such materials. Chlorine bleach is a very powerful caustic chemical and care should be taken in its use. Warning: *Never, never* mix bleach and muriatic acid. This can liberate toxic chlorine gas. Always flush both chemicals well down the drain with excess water when you are done with them.

readers might succumb to the advertising hype of the snake-oil salesmen and purchase such additives. The primary result will be an exchange of currency, not anything particularly beneficial to the artificial ecosystem. If you absolutely *must* buy some brand of this goo, make sure you can purchase a test kit and maintain its concentration at or below the appropriate concentrations found in natural seawater. Concentrations of most of the chemicals found in seawater can be found in references kept at most libraries.

For the most part, the varied life in your reef aquarium will provide its own, rather accurate chemistry. Research chemical additives carefully before you decide to use them in your tank.

Other than *kalkwasser,* the only chemical additive that might have some biological utility is iodine, and there are some supplements available for its addition. Iodine is very toxic, however, and should be added with care. Its concentration in your tank should never exceed that of natural seawater.

Many of the chemicals depleted by organisms in a reef aquarium ecosystem are present in very small amounts and are easily replenished by regular feeding. Most of these trace materials normally are found in low concentrations in normal seawater and are found in the foods derived from natural sources such as plankton or fish. When they enter the aquarium as food, they will be utilized by organisms and maintained at adequate concentrations.

part three

The Organisms

chapter 6

Invertebrates
in Your
Aquarium

Basic Organism Care

Invertebrates have no backbone, but they form the backbone of the beautiful marine reef in your tank. You'll need to look after them well.

There are some useful things to remember about marine reef aquarium organisms that will help you immeasurably in caring for them. All of the organisms found on a reef have evolved over millions of years to survive under the conditions found on the reef. Keeping these organisms at inappropriate temperatures and salinities is the surest way to ensure that they won't survive. The natural and appropriate reef temperatures and salinities have been described in earlier chapters. These are the conditions to which the organisms should be subjected.

The Reef-Keeper's Responsibilities

With very few exceptions, the organisms you have in your care are collected from natural reefs. This has an effect on the reef that may be significant. Reef-keepers have a moral obligation to minimize the potential damage caused by their hobby. To this end, you should purchase captive-bred or -propagated animals if at all possible.

Think twice about keeping a host anemone and clownfish—this is a demanding environment to maintain.

Hobbyists also have the responsibility of researching the organisms they are interested in purchasing. They need to ensure that both their systems and their knowledge are up to the task of maintaining these organisms.

All the organisms for which you will care, with the exception of algae and plants, are animals. All animals need to feed. Many tropical marine animals form a mutualistic relationship or symbiosis with algae called zooxanthellae that live in their tissues. These zooxanthellae provide the animal with a portion of their food but only a portion. It is impossible for these animals to thrive without feeding. All animals need to be fed appropriate foods frequently.

The following section describes some of the common coral reef aquarium organisms. I will try to discuss their special needs and requirements and give some tips about their biological interactions with other organisms.

Invertebrate Animals

With not a little bit of misguided arrogance, humans have divided the animal kingdom into two parts. These parts are the vertebrates, animals like ourselves that have backbones, and the invertebrates, animals lacking backbones. About 3 percent of all described animal species are vertebrates. The remaining 97 percent are invertebrates. Coral reef environments truly are dominated by invertebrates, and most of the animals you will maintain in your aquarium ecosystems simply have to be invertebrates or the system will not be stable.

SCIENTIFIC NAMES AND CLASSIFICATION

Many animals found in the coral reef hobby have no common names and are known only by their scientific names. All scientifically described organisms have a scientific name consisting of two words written in a derived form of Latin. The first word is the name of the genus, and the second word is the name of the species. The name of a common cleaner shrimp is *Stenopus hispidus*; the genus is *Stenopus* and the species is *hispidus*. The genus name always is capitalized but species name never is. Both names are italicized because they are derived from a foreign language (Latin). Several similar species can be found in the same genus. Likewise, similar genera (the plural of genus) are categorized in a bigger group called a family. Many similar families are categorized in an order. Several orders form a class. Finally, all related classes are put into a group called a phylum. (The plural of phylum is phyla.)

A phylum is the first subdivision of the animal kingdom, and it denotes a basic body plan that is unique and different from all other body plans. There are about 35 phyla, each fundamentally distinct and with characteristics all its own. When I discuss aquarium animals, I will give their phylum and class.

Sponges

Sponges belong to the classes Demospongiae and Calcarea, which are classified in the phylum Porifera.

Sponges are the simplest of all animals. They lack tissues, organs and organ systems. A sponge basically is an aggregation of cells that pumps water through itself, filtering bacteria and small particulate material out of the water in the process.

A few sponges have a defined shape, usually tubular, cylindrical or spherical. Most sponges, however, grow as rather amorphous masses.

Sponges are characterized by the presence of irregularly spaced holes in their surface. These holes allow the passage of the water. Sponges also are often characterized by bright colors and can make attractive aquarium additions. The bright colors of sponges, however, often are indicative of the presence of very poisonous chemicals found in their bodies. Bright colors in natural ecosystems with a lot of visual predators typically are warnings to the predators saying, "If you eat me, you will get sick." Many of the fish found on coral reefs are predators that "pick" at the rocks for their food, and the bright colors and chemicals are the way sponges protect themselves. These brightly colored sponges can do well in aquariums, but if they die or are injured, they can release toxic material into the system that causes significant mortality. They often seem to perish because of aquarium system problems. Therefore, it is best to avoid the brilliantly colored sponges until your system is set up and stable.

A sponge's holes allow water to pass in and out of it.

Most sponges have an internal skeleton made of tiny slivers of silica (glass) called spicules. If you use RO/DI water, your water might lack silica. Sponges generally do not do well in such a system. A few sponges possess calcium carbonate skeletons; a few, such as bath sponges, have skeletons made only of protein. These types do well in water lacking silica and can become quite abundant in such tanks.

Corals and Their Kin

Stony corals, soft corals, sea anemones, mushroom polyps, sea fans, hydroids and jellyfish all belong to various subgroups of the phylum Cnidaria, in particular the classes Anthozoa and Hydrozoa. The Cnidaria are characterized by cylindrical bodies that basically are sacks with a single opening, the mouth, at one end. Typically, the mouth is surrounded by tentacles. The number of tentacles varies widely from about eight to several thousand, depending on the species. The inside of the sack is the gut cavity, and all undigested food is expelled back through the mouth because the animals lack a digestive system with an intestine and anus. The animal's body is called a polyp if it lives attached to the substrate, and a medusa or jellyfish if it swims.

The typical coral's mouth is surrounded by flexing tentacles that pull prey in.

HOW CORALS CATCH THEIR PREY

Corals and other members of the phylum Cnidaria have an amazingly sophisticated method of obtaining food. As previously noted, tentacles surround the animals' mouths. The epidermis on the outside of the tentacles is filled with tiny microscopic capsules called nematocysts. Nematocysts are secreted by specialized cells and look like small footballs with a thread coiled inside. They have an amazingly high internal pressure, and when triggered by contact with an appropriate substance, a lid on one end opens and the internal thread is turned inside out and blown out the opening. The thread typically is hollow, and the contents of the capsule often are discharged through it.

The thread penetrates the surface of the prey or whatever the tentacles touch, and the contents of the capsules are blown into the prey. The contents of the capsules often are toxic and kill the prey while the threads hang on to it. The tentacles then flex and pull the prey into the mouth.

STONY CORALS

Stony corals are polyps that secrete an exoskeleton of calcium carbonate in which they live. Although some might leave the exoskeleton if very badly stressed, a phenomenon called polyp bail out, most cannot leave the skeleton. Corals can be found as solitary polyps or as colonies containing between a few polyps and many millions of polyps. In the colonial forms, there are some connections between the guts so that, if one polyp in the colony eats, it is possible for all polyps to get some benefit. The colony form generally is species specific, although it is highly modifiable in different environmental conditions.

Three different categories of stony corals generally are recognized in the aquarium trade. Because none of these categories is a taxonomic category recognized by scientists, there is a significant degree of ambiguity in the groupings. Nonetheless, these are workable groups. The three groups are large polyp corals (LPS), small polyp corals (SPS) and corals without zooxanthellae (*Tubastrea*).

Corals in the first two groups have zooxanthellae that provide them with supplemental nutrition. Because these algae are brownish, the basic color of all stony corals is brown or tan. Obviously, many of these corals also have beautifully colored highlights in

Keep your stony corals colorful by providing bright (and the right) lighting and the proper alkalinity.

shades of red, blue, purple or green. These other colors are created by accessory pigments found in the corals.

There seem to be two major factors in maintaining the bright colors of your corals. The first factor is bright illumination. The brighter corals generally are found in shallow waters with very intense illumination. When put in the average reef tank with much lower levels of light, the coral might thrive, but it typically turns brownish. It is the responsibility of the aquarist to research the needs of his animals and to provide adequately for them. This might include determining that the coral simply cannot maintain its color in your tank because the illumination is not sufficiently intense. The light intensity should *not* include high amounts of ultraviolet light as was thought at one time; excess UV can kill or damage many animals, including humans. Use a UV shield with metal halide bulbs!

The second factor influencing color is the alkalinity of the environment. All corals require both calcium ion and carbonate ion for the calcium carbonate skeleton. Recall that alkalinity also is called carbonate hardness and measures the amount of carbonate ion in the water. The production of brightly colored pigment in some corals seems to require high alkalinity, but the reason for this is unclear.

The zooxanthellae in the corals provide supplemental nutrition for the coral. In natural situations, they can furnish all the caloric requirements a coral needs for short periods. However, the corals soon need other forms of nutrition. In natural conditions, zooxanthellae appear to furnish about 75 percent of the coral's needs. Feeding accounts for about 20 percent, and about 5 percent is derived from the uptake of dissolved materials in the water. In aquariums, these percentages are likely to change significantly. Given the lower light intensities found in our systems, zooxanthellae can be expected to provide about 50 percent of the coral's nutritional needs. Uptake of dissolved material probably provides about 10 to 15 percent, with feeding making up the rest.

It is essential that corals be fed! Feeding provides them with specific materials they can not obtain any other way. A rough rule of thumb for corals and sea anemones is that the size of their tentacles correlates with the size of their food.

Small Polyp Corals

The small polyp corals are most often thought of as reef-forming corals. This large group includes the genera *Acropora, Montipora, Porites, Seriatopora, Pocillopora* and many others. These tend to be most abundant in shallow, wave-swept areas. Generally, they are rapidly growing and often very colorful. The polyps are tiny. This group likely feeds on bacterial aggregates, particulate organic material and invertebrate larvae. They are impossible to directly feed. The presence of a good sand bed in your artificial ecosystem will furnish much of their food, provided the sand bed itself is adequately nourished.

The branches of these corals sometimes can grow as much as a centimeter in length in a month. Corals, like other substrate-dwelling animals, compete actively for their living space. Biological competition is not like competition in sports. The loser doesn't come back next year to try again. The loser in biological competition dies. Corals fight with chemicals and with nematocysts. Consequently, when you stock your tank, plan ahead! If you put your corals too close together, they eventually will fight. Corals that fight are significantly stressed and are prone to several diseases. Once the diseases establish themselves in a tank, they can spread and kill all the corals in the system within a matter of days—even if those corals were not stressed to begin with.

Small polyp corals do best when not competing for space. Leave your corals plenty of room to grow.

Remember, your system should reflect your animals' natural living conditions—in their own habitat, the corals are spread some distance apart. A coral garden with

93

the colonies packed tightly in a tank is a recipe for disaster.

Large Polyp Corals

Large polyp corals, such as species in the genera *Euphyllia, Fungia, Heliofungia, Trachyphyllia, Lobophyllia* and *Caulastrea,* are quite commonly found in home aquariums. These are spectacular animals. The Elegance coral, *Trachyphyllia,* is especially striking.

Mushroom polyps are closely related to stony corals and some scientists consider them to be corals without skeletons.

These animals all have large tentacles and can be fed diced chunks of fish or shrimp. Not all of these animals have the same diet, however. The hobbyist will have to use some foods on a trial-and-error basis to find out what the animals will eat. When you feed them fish or shrimp, make sure you feed the whole animal including the guts. Although we often eat just muscle tissue, most natural predators consume the whole body of the prey and get many essential dietary components this way. Slice or cut up the food into small pieces and use a turkey baster or pipette to place some food on the tentacles or oral disk of the polyp. If the food is acceptable, the animal often will swell up and start to move it to the mouth. If it is unacceptable, it will be sloughed off. When you find an acceptable food source, the corals should be fed at least twice a week. Feeding more often is fine as long as the coral accepts the food.

Large polyp corals all have the capability to produce long sweeper tentacles used in aggression. Some of these corals can reach out 15 to 30 centimeters and can kill other corals, sea anemones or other animals that have the misfortune of being near them. Be careful in your placement of large polyp corals. They fight to win!

Tubastrea

The last grouping of stony corals is the easiest to discuss because there are only a couple corals in this category and both belong to the genus *Tubastrea*. The *Tubastrea* species of brilliant yellow or orange sun corals are those most commonly kept. Unlike most corals found on coral reefs, these species lack zooxanthellae. They are easy to keep, but they require a bit of extra attention. Because they do not have symbiotic algae in their tissues, they must be fed and fed a lot! There might be many polyps and most should be fed at least twice a week. Insufficient feeding is indicated by tissue recession around the bases of the polyps followed by death.

Because they have no symbiotic algae as a food source, the striking Tubastrea *species need to be fed a lot!*

In our tanks, *Tubastrea* species are quite tolerant of fully lit conditions, but they don't seem to be able to resist overgrowth by algae as well as other corals. *Tubastrea* species do best in well-fed, low-light tanks.

SOFT CORALS AND SEA FANS

All soft corals and sea fans are colonial animals that might look superficially like stony corals. They are, however, different types of animals. Unlike stony corals, whose tentacles generally are found in multiples of six, soft corals and sea fans always have eight tentacles and often are called octocorals. The tentacles also have side branches, giving the appearance of a small comb or feather. All of these animals have an internal skeleton made of spicules of calcium carbonate. In some of the animals, such as the sea fans, some of these spicules may be fused with proteinaceous material forming a hard internal core. In others, the spicules are isolated from one another, and the animals are rather floppy and very flexible.

All soft corals and sea fans are specialized to eat small planktonic organisms, although the variety and amount of plankton necessary to keep them alive varies with the species. Many of them have symbiotic algae, and the polyps are the characteristic brownish color of zo-oxanthellate-bearing animals. Other species lack zooxanthellae, and the polyps typically are white or yellow.

The easiest soft corals to keep are the leather corals in the genus *Sarcophyton* and the cabbage corals in the genus *Sinularia*. Each of these will do well in a home reef with effectively no special care necessary. If they start to do well, they will have to be pruned back. This can be done simply by cutting them with a sharp knife.

The branches on the tentacles of soft corals give them a feathery look.

Colonies of *Sarcophyton* can get huge. There are reports of hobbyists having some colonies that weighed more than 150 pounds.

In general, the soft corals do not have virulent nematocysts and compete for space using chemical warfare. Some secrete toxic compounds that are especially harmful to stony corals. If you have a large number of leather corals or a large leather coral in your system, you might find that your stony corals do not grow well or thrive. No amount of filtration will remove those chemicals, so if you suspect the leather coral is retarding the growth of your stony corals, you might want to consider removing it.

Other soft corals such as the "waving hand" or "pulsing" *Xenia* species are largely dependent on their zooxanthellae for nutrition and might not feed at all. Given good water conditions, these animals tend to grow rapidly and can produce a lot of daughter colonies. They require a bit of current and moderate light but little in the way of other specific care.

Sea Anemones and Their Kin

The remaining members of the phylum Cnidaria commonly found in reef tanks are animals that can be loosely referred to as sea anemones and their close relatives. Sea anemones can be thought of as corals without skeletons that have an adhesive foot used for attachment and slow crawling. They all have tentacles used for prey capture.

The bumps on a mushroom polyp are its tentacles.

MUSHROOM POLYPS

Mushroom polyps, scientifically known as Coralliomorph sea anemones, are very much like corals without a skeleton. Their adhesive disk is small, and they do not move much nor can they reattach easily. They typically have a large, flat oral disk with a lot of warts and bumps on it. These warts and bumps are their tentacles. The animals vary in size up to about the size of a dinner plate. These big polyps, in the genus *Actinodiscus,* are predators of fish and are quite effective at catching and consuming fish in an aquarium. They make fascinating inhabitants of a reef system, but they should be kept in an all-invertebrate tank or with fish specifically designated as disposable.

Smaller mushroom polyps are available in a wide variety of colors and tentacle patterns. Most seem to fare best under low to moderate light intensities. They eat occasionally if fed, but they often seem to not pay any attention to food put on their disks. If conditions are good, they will grow and reproduce by budding off new individuals, and they are quite good at filling empty space in their little corner of the world.

SEA MATS

Feed sea mats food appropriate to the size of their disks.

Sea mats, or zooanthids, can be thought of as colonial sea anemones. Depending on the variety, they might or might not be able to easily separate to form individuals. Most kept in home tanks have zooxanthellae, but all will benefit from feeding. The size of the food they can take is proportional to the size of the oral disk. Try a number of different foods to find which ones give the best result in terms of growth and reproduction. They reproduce by budding new individuals in the mat, causing the mat to enlarge.

SEA ANEMONES

Sea anemones are not colonial, although large aggregations can be found in a few species. Most sea anemones found in tropical reef tanks have zooxanthellae. The most common species without zooxanthellae is the Giant Caribbean Anemone, *Condylactis gigantea.* This species is basically white, but it often has pale tints of green, pink or yellow. It probably is the easiest of the large anemones to maintain. The Giant Caribbean Anemone likes to put its foot and column in a rock crevice and inflate and extend from the hole. It must be fed frequently, and it eats a number of foods. It gets rather large, up to about 20 centimeters across, but most aquarium specimens are much smaller.

The Giant Caribbean Anemone is frequently kept by hobbyists.

Several sea anemone species are collectively called host anemones because they serve as natural hosts to one or more species of symbiotic clownfish. Almost every aquarist wants to maintain some clownfish on a host anemone. This is not something that should be attempted by beginners. These anemones are difficult to maintain and will perish if put into a newly set up tank. None of these animals has been bred in captivity, and the aquarium trade is seriously reducing their populations in some areas. Every anemone collected for the aquarium trade means the loss of a natural clownfish habitat. The anemones have poor reproductive success, probably due to significant juvenile mortality. Once they pass through the hazardous period, however, they can live for a very long time. Age estimates range upward of several centuries. It is a crime against nature to collect and transport animals that old and then provide incorrect conditions for them in a reef aquarium so they die in a matter of days, weeks or months.

In the right hands, these animals are not hard to keep in an established tank. They need an aquarium substrate that mimics their natural habitat, excellent water conditions, lots of food and good lighting. Given these conditions, they generally will thrive. If you must have one of these animals, wait until your system has been established for at least 6 months. Research the conditions necessary for their health and try to purchase a healthy animal.

All of these animals have zooxanthellae, so the basic ground color of healthy animals is tan, brownish or greenish-gray. Animals that are bright white generally are doomed, although occasionally with proper feeding they can live long enough to reestablish their population of zooxanthellae. Look for animals responsive to touch and shadows and look for animals that hold their mouth tightly closed. These conditions indicate good health.

Host anemones get large, and they are very aggressive. Some actively hunt down and kill other anemones in their tank. They move around slowly but can exert tremendous hydraulic forces with their pedal disk as they move. They can seriously disrupt a set-up reef tank and can kill lots of other animals by either stinging them or simply moving over them. A happy anemone, however, is a stationary anemone; if they have the right conditions, they generally will stay put and thrive. Once the anemone is stable and has been living well for a few months, clownfish can be introduced.

A final group of smaller anemone species deserves attention. These are anemones in the genus *Aiptasia*, variously known as the glass anemone, the sand anemone, the rock anemone or more appropriately as the plague anemone. There may be more than four species in this group, but they all look alike. They are tan or gray, often with banded tentacles and a few white radial marks on

> ## BEWARE OF COLORFUL HOST ANEMONES
>
> Do not, under any circumstances, purchase a host anemone that is brightly colored. Dying these animals is a barbarous procedure practiced by some collectors and importers. They collect anemones and put them in a dark tank for several weeks until all the zooxanthellae are killed. They then inject the animals with yellow, red or blue dye and ship them out for export. Such animals are doomed, and they generally live no longer than a few weeks. If aquarists quit buying such animals, this unnecessary killing of beautiful creatures can be curtailed.

the disk. Large ones can be 10 centimeters high with a tentacle span of about 8 centimeters. They thrive in reef aquariums, prolifically reproducing asexually by budding and pedal laceration. One large adult can produce 30 to 50 offspring a week. They have virulent strings and will kill and overgrow corals, soft corals and just about any other animal in the system.

There are several methods of *Aiptasia* eradication, all of which work sporadically, including injection with hot kalkwasser paste, bleach or muriatic acid. The use of biological controls such as copper-banded butterfly fish or peppermint shrimp, *Lysmata wurdemanni*, can help. Unfortunately, all of these methods have problems. Probably the easiest way to control *Aiptasia* is by adding an animal that eats them. Recently, a small sea slug or nudibranch, *Berghia verucornis*, has been found that feeds only on *Aiptasia* and that reproduces well in the home aquarium. In at least some situations, it has indeed eradicated the plague, and it might be the best bet for control of these pests.

Aiptasia *is a sea anemone that will take over your tank. Make an effort to keep it out of your aquarium.*

It is easiest to kill the pest anemone on live rock before it is put into the main tank. For this reason, it is prudent to have a smaller tank in which you can place the live rock you purchase. Each piece should be placed in the tank and carefully examined. Any small tannish or grey sea anemones should be killed using *kalkwasser* paste or bleach injected into them with a syringe, and all traces of their bodies should be removed. The rock then can be thoroughly rinsed and put into the tank. A bit of work at this stage can save a *lot* of grief in the future.

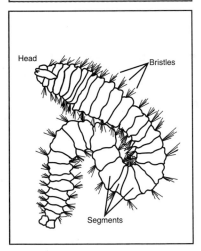

Head
Bristles
Segments

A full-grown fireworm can reach 16 inches in length. Fireworms are fine little scavengers—just leave them alone.

Bristle Worms

Shortly after an artificial reef ecosystem is established, every aquarist notices there are worms in it, sometimes quite large ones. Most aquarists greet this appearance with profound disgust and fear. This is unfortunate; these worms generally are members of the scavenging guild of animals necessary for the appropriate functioning of the sand bed and other components of the ecosystem.

These bristle worms, or polychaetes, are members of the class Polychaeta in the phylum Annelida. They are marine relatives of the common earthworm. They differ from earthworms in that they can have a lot of appendages on their bodies. There is much variety in this group, and it is hard to make many generalizations, but most of them have visible flaps or appendages on each side of each segment. They also might have any number of tentacles, or feelers, on the head or elsewhere.

The most common worms that appear in our systems are fireworms, or Amphinomids. These typically are pink, and each segment has a large evident tuft of white bristles on each side. These bristles are much like those of a porcupine; they are sharpened barbs designed to break off and stay in the skin of a predator. They also contain a chemical irritant so that they hurt if you get them in your skin.

Although one species of fireworm occasionally preys on soft corals, it is almost never seen in reef tanks. Most of the species that show up in reef tanks are beneficial scavengers. They reproduce well in aquariums and live in burrows in the rocks or sand. They can become quite large, up to about 20 centimeters in length.

Numerous other smaller worms can be seen on the sediments or rocks. Spirorbids constitute one of the most easily recognizable of these species. They often are first noticed on the walls of the aquarium as tiny, white, calcareous spirals. They grow on all hard substrates but are never much more than ⅛-inch across. If you examine one through the wall using a magnifying glass, a small tuft of red, filter-feeding tentacles can be seen.

Feather duster worms, such as these Christmas tree worms, need a well-established tank to thrive. Wait at least a year before adding them to your aquarium.

FEATHER DUSTER WORMS

Hobbyists often are tempted to purchase feather duster polychaetes. They generally purchase one of two types: the giant feather dusters, *Sabellastarte magnifica,* or Christmas tree worms, *Spirobranchus giganteus.* Neither is really a good choice for a beginning tank. Both of these species need a significant amount of microplankton to survive, and such microplankton don't generally develop in an artificial reef ecosystem until it has been set up for a year or more.

Crustaceans

Many crustaceans of the phylum Arthropoda and sub-phylum Crustacea can be found in a mini-reef aquarium. Most are desirable, and many show up on the live rock or in the live sand. The most important of these are the microcrustaceans or, as they generally are known by aquarists, "tiny bugs." There are two or three types of minute crustaceans that hopefully will become abundant in every artificial reef ecosystem. They are important for several reasons:

- They form a major component of the scavengers.
- They produce a large part of the microplankton of the system during their reproduction.
- They are an important component of the diet of many fish and invertebrates.

A view from above of a female harpaticoid copepod. These tiny animals often are seen as white specks moving around the walls of a newly established tank.

The two most commonly seen microcrustaceans are harpacticoid copepods and amphipods. Harpacticoids are really tiny—about the size of the tip of a pin—and generally are seen in great abundance as small white moving specks on the walls of the aquarium about two to three weeks after it has been established. With a magnifying glass, you can see that they are basically tear-drop shaped and that they move with a jerky motion. Many have a second dot attached to the back end. Each of these is a female with a cluster of eggs attached to her abdomen. The copepod populations are reduced significantly after the first fish are added to the system, but they always persist in a well-fed tank.

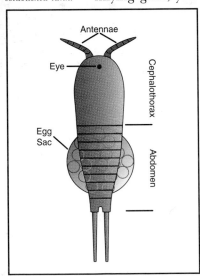

The other variety of important crustaceans are the amphipods. These can reach up to about ½ inch in length, but most are much smaller. They tend to be C-shaped when swimming or crawling on the glass, and their legs come out of the opening of the C. They also are flattened a bit from side to side. These are most frequently seen at night when they come out to forage on the rocks.

Both types of crustaceans eat detritus, algae or particulate organic material. Both are necessary components of the scavenger group of animals that builds up in the system, and both make good fish food.

SHRIMPS

Numerous shrimp are available as additions to the fauna of the reef aquarium. Several of these species are desirable and very attractive. Probably the best-known shrimp is the cleaner shrimp. In nature, these shrimp are found at "cleaning stations," where they stay in sight for fish to see. They have long white antennae that are quite visible and that signal to fish that they are present. Fish approach them and allow the shrimp to clean parasites from their bodies. If parasitized fish are rare, the shrimp are also good scavengers.

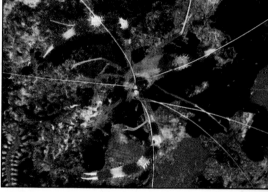

Banded Coral Shrimp

The largest of the cleaner shrimp species is *Stenopus hispidus,* the banded coral shrimp. These are strikingly colored, large and active animals that make a good addition to an artificial reef ecosystem. They can reach several inches in length. Banded coral shrimp generally are sold as solitary animals or as mated pairs and should not be purchased any other way. The females are larger than the males and can be three or four times the size of their consorts. They are quite territorial, and a large female generally will not tolerate another female in the tank with her. They will fight to the death. They might be aggressive toward other shrimps and crustaceans as well, but this rarely is a serious problem. Some individuals do pick up the bad habit of pulling food out of anemones or corals, but this can be avoided by giving the shrimp some food first.

Colorful banded coral shrimp are fine members of the community tank as long as you keep only one female. The females are territorial and often fight to the death.

Scarlet Cleaner Shrimp

Scarlet cleaner shrimps, *Lysmata ambioensis,* also are beautiful additions to the system. They are smaller than the *Stenopus* and are not nearly as aggressive. They are best kept in breeding pairs. If they are fed sufficiently, they will produce a batch of eggs every two weeks or so. Hobbyists have never been able to raise the young, but the larvae provide good food for the plankton feeders in the tanks. They have a peculiar life history, which includes the alternation of gender. The female will release her eggs, molt (shed her exoskeleton), and change into a male. It then mates with another shrimp that has just molted and turned into a female. That shrimp deposits its eggs in a greenish mass under the abdomen. It will release them in two weeks, molt and the cycle will continue. If they are fed well, each individual of the pair will molt about every two weeks.

Peppermint Shrimp

Peppermint shrimp, *Lysmata wurdemanni,* often are purchased and put into reef systems to help eat the plague anemones, *Aiptasia.* Peppermint shrimp are largely nocturnal and generally are not visible during the lighted hours of the system. They forage at night, and some aquarists have had success with them controlling the anemones. If there are not appropriate anemones around, they also are good scavengers. Some individuals eat other sea anemones, sea mats or corals, however, and might not be a welcome addition to all tanks.

CRABS

With only a few exceptions, crabs are not reef-safe. Most are essentially predatory and can cause problems in the systems.

Hermit Crabs

Small hermit crabs, such as the blue-legged hermits, *Pagurus tricolor,* make useful additions to a reef system. These animals act as highly mobile scavengers and eat a lot of algae, helping to control filamentous algae outbreaks. Generally, you should add about one or two of these small crabs per gallon of tank volume. They generally don't seem to bother any other tank inhabitants. In addition to their cleaning functions, they have a lot of interesting behaviors. It often is beneficial to purchase some extra shells for them at the same time they are added.

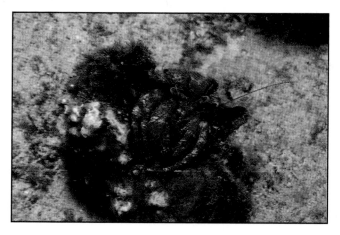

Many hermit crabs, such as the Dardanus venosus, *can be destructive in your tank. It's better to avoid these crabs rather than to take chances.*

A number of other hermit crab species are offered for sale under these names: scarlet hermits, red-legged hermits, Mexican red legs, and so on. None of these has been shown to be reef-safe, and a number of them are decidedly predatory. These predators eat snails, other hermits, shrimp and fish. They should be avoided.

Other Good Reef Crabs

One of the safe crabs is the emerald crab, *Mithrax sculptus*. This mostly herbivorous crab is useful in controlling some types of potential algal pests.

The safest crabs for the aquarium probably are the anemone or porcelain crabs. These crabs generally are filter-feeders and can be seen straining water through a pair of modified mouth parts they wave in the water. They make fascinating tank inhabitants, but they need a tank with lots of plankton for long-term survival. Wait until your tank is at least six months to one year old before adding anemone crabs. Arrow crabs, *Stenorhynchus seticornus*, also are acceptable as tank inhabitants when they are small. They scavenge on excess food and eat polychaete worms. Reports of larger ones tearing apart corals or anemones to get the food they have eaten are relatively common, yet some individuals do not do this.

Mollusks

Mollusks are members of the phylum Mollusca and are an amazingly successful group of animals. They are common and successful in coral reefs, and many of them make desirable additions to our systems.

Clams

Clams are a type of mollusk in the class Bivalvia. Only one type of clam is appropriate for reef aquarium ecosystems, the giant clams of the genera *Tridacna* and *Hippopus*. All other clams, such as flame scallops, thorny oysters, and pen shells, eat small phytoplankton. It is impossible to maintain sufficient phytoplankton in our systems to keep these other species alive. With appropriate care, however, the giant clams will thrive.

Giant clams need strong lighting to do well in a home aquarium (Tridacna crocea).

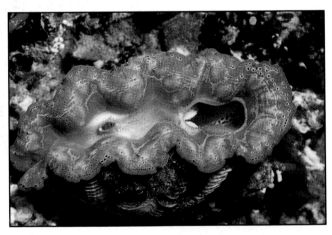

Giant clams all have zooxanthellae in them, similar to hermatypic corals. The zooxanthellae are found in the expanded mantle tissue and provide much of the clam's nutrition. The clams still need to feed, however, and fare best in a well-established system with good sand bed fauna. The clams require a *lot* of light to do well and should not be put into any system without metal halide lighting. There are several species of *Tridacna*, and the care of each kind is somewhat different. Be aware that these animals are particularly prone to attacks from some parasitic snails. Specialized references about the care of these beautiful animals should be consulted prior to purchasing one of these clams.

Snails

Snails are categorized in the class Gastropoda. A complement of the appropriate algae-eating snails is necessary for the success of the artificial reef ecosystem. Many different types of snails are acceptable, and all of them will do the job just fine. These animals graze the diatom film on the walls and rocks in the aquarium and assist in the passage of nutrients through the ecosystem. Some of the acceptable types of snails that can be used for this task include *Astraea, Turbo, Haliotis* (Abalone), *Nerita, Cerithium* and *Stomatella.* Given the diversity of the snail groups, there are likely many more species that also fit the bill for algal control.

Snails contribute to the ecological balance of your reef tank (Astraea sp.).

All snails are very sensitive to changes in salinity and need to be acclimated very slowly to prevent significant mortality. Acclimation times of three to five hours are necessary to ensure survival. During this period, the salinity of the snail's container is slowly adjusted to match that of the tank it is entering.

Starfish and Related Animals

Starfish, sea urchins, brittle stars and sea cucumbers are all members of the phylum Echinodermata. Unfortunately, the choices of reef-safe echinoderms, however, is severely limited. All echinoderms are severely stressed by changes in salinity, and all *need* to be kept at full-strength seawater.

STARFISH

Only one species of starfish, or sea star, can do well in a reef aquarium without eating many of the other inhabitants. That animal is the blue star, *Linckia laevigata.* This starfish appears to dine on detritus and bacterial films in the reef and is harmless to other animals. No other star offered for sale in the reef trade is really reef-safe.

BRITTLE OR SERPENT STARS

Numerous species of brittle or serpent stars can do well in reef aquariums, but some are definitely predatory on other tank inhabitants. Generally, smaller species are safe, as are black, white and red stars. A beautiful green brittle star with gold or yellow markings on it, *Ophioarachna incrassata,* should be avoided at all costs. It catches and eats fish, shrimp and other invertebrates and tears corals and sea anemones apart to get the food they have eaten. Most of the other brittle stars make good scavengers and are attractive additions to the reef. You can thwart predatory tendencies by offering them a piece of fish or shrimp at feeding times.

Reef-safe sea urchins include the boring urchin, Echinomerta lucunter.

SEA URCHINS

Sea urchins often are useful animals in the control of pest algae, particularly the smaller short-spined urchins such as the blue-tuxedo urchin, *Mespilia globulus.* Larger urchins often are bulldozers and occasionally knock over rocks and other livestock. Long-spined urchins such as the *Diadema* species are good for algae control, but the long spines are venom-tipped and can inflict a nasty wound if you are a bit careless around them.

Pencil urchins such as the common Caribbean *Eucidaris tribuloides*, which often is for sale, are carnivores. They not only eat immobile animals, such as soft corals and sea mats, they also have an amazing capability to catch and eat fish and shrimp. They also are largely nocturnal and are significantly capable of rearranging the rocks in a tank. They are not reef-safe and should be avoided.

SEA CUCUMBERS

Some sea cucumbers are good additions to reef systems, particularly the generally ugly, sand-mopping and burrowing sea cucumbers. Likewise, some of the filter-feeding cukes are good reef aquarium inhabitants. Take care, however, to avoid the sea apples. These are brightly colored and relatively large sea cucumbers that crawl on surfaces in the aquarium and feed on materials in the water. They are loaded with poisons, and if they are stressed in any manner, they tend to release the poisons into the tank. Avoid grief and don't buy these animals!

HANDLE WITH CARE

Most of the Cnidarians found in the aquarium hobby are not dangerous to the aquarist, but a few might be. The virulence of the venom and the size of the nematocysts are not related to the size of the animal nor to the basic types of animals. When handling some Cnidarians, particularly sea anemones, hydroids and jellyfish, you can get a painful sting.

All Cnidarians should be handled with caution. Even if you don't feel a sting when they touch you, the nematocysts are likely discharging into your skin. It is best to take precautions when handling the animals to avoid being touched.

chapter 7

Fishes and Algae
in Your
Aquarium

Fishes are vertebrates (phylum Chordata) in the class of animals known as Osteichthyes. The number of fish species found on coral reefs seems limitless, and many of them are imported for the aquarium trade. These fishes often do better in fish-only tanks than in artificial reef ecosystems. Fishes need to be chosen very carefully prior to introduction. Once placed in a well-established reef, it can be effectively impossible to capture them without dismantling the whole reef.

Good Reef Tank Fishes

Although you should make sure to select your fishes very thoughtfully, many species of fish tend to make good tank inhabitants.

TANGS

Most tangs are herbivorous and will act to control algae in a system. Confined in a small tank, they often remove all the filamentous and foliose algae. Of course, they still need to be fed. Tangs typically are colorful, active fish whose presence will add a lot to a reef aquarium ecosystem.

Most tangs are welcome additions to your coral reef ecosystem (Indian ocean sailfin tang, Zebrasoma desjardinii).

BLENNIES

Many blennies are good reef aquarium inhabitants, specifically the mostly herbivorous species such as the bicolor blenny or the red-lipped blenny. They will eat diatoms off the rocks and aquarium walls as well as eating bits of offered vegetable matter. They typically do well in coral reef aquariums.

DAMSELFISH

Damselfish of just about any sort make good reef inhabitants, although they tend to be aggressive and territorial. After damselfish have been introduced to a system and have set up their territories, it often is difficult to introduce other fish into the tank. The damsels might attack them repeatedly and even kill them. Damselfish also set up a pecking order among themselves. It often is better to have a group of four or five fish rather than just a pair because the dominance responses are diffused over more fish.

CLOWNFISH

Clownfish are a popular addition to the reef tank and don't need a host anemone in captivity.

Clownfish (or anemone fish) are some of the most striking and personable of marine fish. They are strongly territorial and make good aquarium pets. In a tank of less than 200 gallons, it is not a good idea to try to keep more than a pair of one species. In nature, clownfish always are found with a host anemone; in aquariums, however, they don't need anemones in which to reside. They will set up residence in a cave, a coral or a non-

host anemone. In both host anemones and other substitute cnidarians, clownfish will rub themselves frequently with the slime of the host. This seems to prevent the host from discharging its nematocysts into them. Clownfish spawn frequently, and it is easy to raise the offspring.

Dottybacks are territorial fish. Some bear a strong resemblance to royal grammas, and the fish often are misidentified.

DOTTYBACKS

The colorful fishes known as dottybacks make attractive tank inhabitants. They are territorial, and like other territorial fishes, they tend to be aggressive. Occasionally, some individuals of most of these species can become nuisance fish that attack and kill shrimps and other crustaceans.

WRASSES

Many wrasses make good tank inhabitants, although some of them develop a taste for their neighbors. In particular, smaller snails and crustaceans are at risk of being eaten by these fish. The wrasses' swimming behavior and beautiful color, however, may compensate for their predatory habits.

LIONFISH

The spectacular lionfish are members of the group called scorpion fishes. They have venom glands at the bases of their long, flowing fins. Lionfish often are kept by hobbyists, and they make good aquarium pets provided the dangerous and toxic nature of their spines are appreciated. An inadvertent jab by a spine can be excruciating and can seriously ruin your whole day. Lionfish eat other fishes, and anything smaller than themselves is considered a food item. Most can be trained to take foods other than live foods, but any other smaller tank inhabitants are potential snacks.

The rule for the lionfish is "look but don't touch" (Volitans lionfish, Pterois volitans).

DRAGONETS

The group of fishes known as the dragonets have several members that make great aquarium pets. They have specialized diets, however, and unless certain conditions are met, they will starve to death. The most popular of this group is the Mandarin goby. These small fishes truly are spectacular with their blue, green and orange coloration. Mandarin fish eat very tiny crustaceans and protozoa living on the rocks or in the algae found in the aquarium and they can only survive in a tank with a lot of live rock or a tank in which algal growth is luxuriant.

Fishes to Avoid

The fishes that are not really acceptable for coral reef aquariums include virtually all of the angelfishes. In addition to having dietary requirements that are difficult for the hobbyist to supply, the larger angels simply get too big for humane care in any hobbyist tank. The pygmy angels in the *Centropyge* group generally are nipping predators on sessile invertebrates and corals. Confined in the small volume of an aquarium, they generally become significant predators on a few of the organisms and will kill them.

Pygmy angelfish, such as the flame angelfish, are likely to nip at your corals. They are best kept only in sizable tanks.

Generally, butterfly fishes cause the same problems as the small angels. Most of them are coral or soft coral predators, and most will not adapt to alternative food sources. Placed in an aquarium, they either will eat all the other animals in the aquarium and then starve to death, or they will simply starve to death. These are animals that should be avoided.

Algae

Several types of algae commonly appear in our artificial ecosystems. Marine algae and spores are in the air all around us. Live diatoms, for example, have been collected in air samples at high altitudes over the central part of North America. These inocula might occasionally start a growth in a tank. Most of the algae, however, enter with the live materials put into the tank.

An alga's color provides a relatively easy way to distinguish it, so let's look at some algae.

BLUE-GREEN ALGAE

Blue-green algae, or cyanobacteria, are bacteria with a photosynthetic capability. They are called algae, but they are not related at all to any of the other organisms called algae. These organisms all have accessory pigments that mask the basic green color of chlorophyll, giving them colors that range from black to blue-green to a reddish-purple. Cyanobacteria are absolutely essential to the well-being of your artificial reef. They live in the sediments, metabolize dissolved organic material and in turn are eaten by worms, protozoans and other micro-predators.

> ### WHAT ARE ALGAE
>
> Except for some of the green algae, none of the photosynthetic organisms in a typical reef tank are classified as plants by scientists. Most are only superficially plant-like.

Some cyanobacteria, however, occasionally might be found on the substrate surfaces of your system. They can grow on rocks, aquarium walls, sediments or even completely over animals such as corals. These particular organisms have the common name of red slime algae and form a slimy reddish or purplish film. In extreme cases, the oxygen produced by photosynthesis forms internal bubbles and causes the whole mass to lift up a bit off the substrate. These mats of cyanobacteria are caused by an overabundance of nutrients in the water, which is caused by insufficient animals in the scavenger guilds and reduced fauna in the live sand. The nutrient abundance also is facilitated by a lack of other photosynthetic organisms that might be able to use the nutrients. Cyanobacteria growth can be exceptionally rapid. They can form thick mats in a matter of hours.

Blue-green algae are an essential component of a reef tank's sediment.

Caulerpa and other large algae can be added to your tank to help eliminate an over-abundance of blue-green algae.

Their growth also is facilitated by low currents, and they often are found in "dead" spots where debris and detritus accumulate and decompose to produce dissolved nutrients.

These patches and mats can be eliminated by a series of actions. First, they should be siphoned from the tank, and a partial water change should be done to reduce the dissolved-nutrient concentration. Feeding frequency or amounts should be cut back to allow some of the dissolved material to make its way out of the system through the live sand fauna. Some larger algae such as *Caulerpa* should be established to assist in the removal

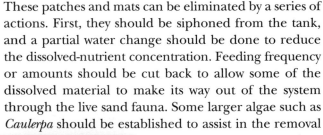

of nutrients. The cyanobacteria themselves are not eaten by many organisms. It usually takes about one month to get an outbreak under control. If you've cut back on feeding levels, normal levels can then be resumed.

There are chemical treatments that involve using an antibiotic to reduce the levels of cyanobacteria, and they do work. They do nothing, however, to reduce the root cause of the outbreak. As soon as the antibiotic decomposes, the outbreak will continue. It is better to attack the real causes of the outbreak than to go for the quick fix.

GOLDEN ALGAE

Golden algae, or diatoms, are unicellular algae that live in a secreted shell composed of silica. Both planktonic and benthic diatoms can be found in artificial systems, but planktonic diatoms are much more abundant in nature than in the home aquarium. Benthic diatoms, however, are common. They are minute and are individually invisible; however, they are capable of rapid growth and are found in reef tanks as the brownish or yellow-brown film that grows on the walls of the aquarium and over the rocks or the substrates. These organisms are found in natural systems, and it is virtually impossible to remove them from aquaria. We don't want to remove them, however, because they are a vital part of the food webs utilizing dissolved nutrients. They can be controlled by adding herbivorous grazers, such as several species of marine snails, to the system.

BROWN JELLY OR SNOT ALGAE

Brown jelly algae also are known as dinoflagellates. This is another group of small, unicellular algae. They are absolutely necessary for the proper development of an artificial reef because zooxanthellae are symbiotic dinoflagellates that live in corals, tridacnid clams and other animals.

Occasionally, however, there are outbreaks of dinoflagellates that might cover all surfaces in our aquarium with a brownish mucoid layer. Fortunately, these algal blooms are relatively rare; unfortunately, there is no easy cure for them. The mucoid material, literally billions of small algal cells imbedded in a gelatinous mucus, should be siphoned out of the system, and a 50 percent water change should be done to remove excess nutrients. The lighting intensity and photoperiod should be reduced as well.

After the excess nutrient level in the water is reduced, more live sand and scavengers should be added and feeding should be reduced until the sand becomes noticeably populated with fauna. At that time, the system should be stable and further blooms are unlikely.

GREEN ALGAE

Green algae include most of the algal organisms of concern to aquarists. Numerous varieties are grown or are added to the aquarium as "decorative algae." Others hitchhike in on live rock; still others are common problem algae that grow as unwanted weeds.

Most of the algae found on a natural coral reef are coralline green algae. These are green algae that deposit calcium carbonate inside their tissues. In natural situations, most of these algae grow like a crust over all the rocks and rubble, cementing it together. They are truly responsible for the reef because they form the solid substrate out of coral rubble and debris. About 80 percent of all living tissue on the natural reef is algal.

Suspension-feeding organisms will eat some of the gametes, and protein skimming can remove many as well.

Caulerpa

Decorative green algae include species in the Caulerpa *genus.*

The most commonly added decorative green algae are in the genus *Caulerpa*. There are numerous species or varieties of these algae with different shapes of the algal blades, and many of them are strikingly interesting. In a well-fed aquarium, they often grow well utilizing the dissolved organic material in the water. Consequently, they are useful as a way to remove excess organic material. They can be harvested periodically, and often can be traded or sold to a local aquarium store, removing significant amounts of nutrients.

Halimeda

The calcareous green algal genus *Halimeda* has several species commonly seen in marine aquariums. These often are referred to as "cactus algae" and are rather desirable tank inhabitants because their growth indicates good water quality. They grow out from the substrate as a series of linked tissue segments as hardened calcium carbonate. They reproduce similarly to *Caulerpa* and need to be pruned occasionally. If they reproduce, the white calcareous plates will fall to the bottom and will eventually be integrated into the sediment bed.

GREEN CORALLINE ALGAE

Green coralline algae often are found in reef tanks. They are rather obscure on rocks because they often are the same gray to gray-green color of the base rock. They frequently start to grow on the aquarium walls, however, and become noticeable as green circular patches. Such algae are difficult to remove from the walls of an acrylic tank, but they can be removed easily with a razorblade from the walls of a glass tank.

In moderation, bubble algae is considered decorative.

BUBBLE ALGAE

Bubble algae, several species of the genus *Valonia*, look like green bubbles that grow on the rocks and elsewhere in the tank. One species from the Caribbean, *Valonia ventricose*, gets fairly large—up to the size of a walnut. It often gets a silvery appearance and is rather attractive. A few smaller species look like fat green tubes or tiny sausages that grow over rocks. These are not flaccid or filmy algae, rather they are tough organisms; it is rather difficult to puncture one, for example. In most cases, they grow slowly and offer interesting decoration. In many cases, however, they can spread rapidly and can even overgrow corals. If they appear to be on their way to being a problem in your system, they can be controlled by the addition of an emerald crab, *Mithrax sculptus*, to the system. The crab will eat them.

Hair Algae

Other types of problem green algae include several species collectively known as hair algae. These grow in tufts that look, as their name indicates, like green hair. If left uncontrolled, they can overgrow large portions of the system and are rather unsightly. They can be relatively hard to manage, but they can be kept at bay by utilizing a combination of predation, mostly by the small blue-legged hermit crab, and competition from the more decorative green algae. I generally leave a clump or two of the hair algae growing in an obscure part of one of my systems. These clumps are some of the prime foods and habitats for small crustaceans that are food for a pair of Mandarin dragonets found in that system.

Coralline red algae usually grows well in the home reef tank.

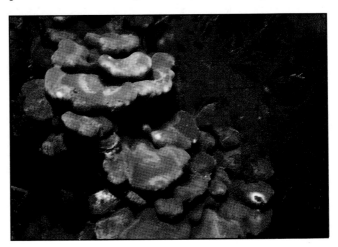

RED ALGAE

One algal group is desired by most reef aquarists—the coralline red algae. There are many species of coralline red algae, and they generally grow as crusts over the rock substrate. The colors range from delicate pinks to striking lavenders and crimsons. In natural situations, these algae are found in caves, under rocks, in shaded areas or in deep water. Their red pigments are accessory photopigments that assist the chlorophyll by absorbing some of the blue light found in shaded situations. Coralline red algae are not found in naturally well-lit areas; they are replaced by coralline green algae.

Perhaps the ease with which these algae grow in the home tank is a reflection of the relatively low light intensities found in our artificial ecosystems as compared to the real world.

Coralline red algae are introduced to the system by the use of live rock. Colorful live rock from tropical areas have algae on them that will grow well in your system and that might spread to cover parts of the walls and hardware as well.

Numerous types of red macroalgae will thrive in the reef tank, and occasionally some nice specimens will grow from live rock. Foliose red algae, in contrast to green algae, is hard to transplant because it attaches to rocks with a different type of adhesion. Consequently, it is hard to purchase some of these algae from a dealer, get them home and have them stay put in a system. The best hope of maintaining some foliose red macroalgae is to have some sprout from live rock you've added.

Beyond the
Basics

part four

Beyond
the
Basics

chapter 8

Recommended
Reading and
Resources

Books

Adey, Walter and Karen Loveland. *Dynamic Aquaria: Building Living Ecosystems.* Academic Press, 1998.

Borneman, Eric H. and J.E.N. Veron. *Aquarium Coral: An Illustrated Handbook for the Reef Aquarist.* Microcosm, Ltd., 1999.

Dakin, Nick. *The Marine Aquarium Problem Solver.* Tetra Press, 1996.

Delbeek, J. Charles and Julian Sprung. *The Reef Aquarium: A Comprehensive Guide to the Identification and Care of Tropical Marine Invertebrates Vol. I: Stony Corals and Tridacna Clams,* Coconut Grove, FL: Ricordia Pub., 1994.

Fenner, Robert M. *The Conscientious Marine Aquarist.* Microcosm Ltd., 1998.

Knop, Donald. *Giant Clams: A Comprehensive Guide to the Identification and Care of Tridacnid Clams.* Two Little Fishes, 1996.

Michael, Scott W. *Reef Fishes, Volume 1: A Guide to Their Identification, Behavior and Captive Care.* Microcosm Ltd., 1998.

Moe, Martin A. Jr. *The Marine Aquarium Handbook: Beginner to Breeder.* Green Turtle Publications, 1992.

Moe, Martin A. Jr. *The Marine Aquarium Reference: Systems and Invertebrates.* Green Turtle Publications, 1993.

Puterbaugh, Ed and Eric Borneman. *A Practical Guide to Corals for the Reef.* Crystal Publications, 1997.

Tullock, John H. *Your First Marine Aquarium.* Hauppauge, NY: Barron's Educational Series, Inc., 1998.

Tullock, John H. *Natural Reef Aqauriums.* Microcosm Ltd., 1997.

Tullock, John H. *Clownfishes and Sea Anemones.* Hauppauge, NY: Barron's Educational Series, Inc., 1998.

Magazines

Aquarium Fish
Fancy Publications, Inc.
P.O. Box 6050
Mission Viejo, CA 92690

Today's Aquarist
Pisces Publishing Group, Inc.
417 Bridgeport Ave.
Devon, CT 06460-4105

Tropical Fish Hobbyist
TFH
One TFH Plaza
Neptune City, NJ 07753

Articles

Hamner, et al. 1988. "Zooplankton, planktivorous fish and water currents on a windward reef face, Great Barrier Reef, Australia." *Bulletin of Marine Science.* 42:459–478.

Online Magazines

Aquarium Frontiers Online (Fancy Publications, Inc.) www.aquariumfrontiers.com

Aquarium.Net (Rick Martin, Publisher) www.aquarium.net

Websites

http://garf.org/news   Reef Aquarium Farming News, an online newsletter for reef aquarium propagation research.

http://132.239.112.5/SBAM2/sbam_000   Birch Aquarium at Scripp's Institute of Oceanography.

www.fishlinkcentral.com   Fishlink Central, a site that provides extensive resources.